MW00449597

“My fellow LBC girl Tiffani showin her mad cooking skills in this new book that’s all about leftovers. And ya know ya boy gets the munchies pretty often so what better way to feed tha need than with these cool recipes made from leftovers . . . I loves me some leftovers. But even if you don’t like to cook . . . just buy the book.”

—SNOOP DOGG, or Calvin as Tiffani knows me

“Tiffani Thiessen has created the book that every parent, every first-time cook, every household of one, every cook with housemates, lovemates, and every family NEEDS to have in their kitchen. I am all here for the mashed potato dumplings (I learned a new trick that my family loves) and spaghetti pie and all the rest of the amazing recipes, but going to 5,000 feet above sea level, a book this fun, so keenly photographed, with such yummy food, is so important in a world where 40 percent of what comes into our food pipeline gets wasted. This cookbook, born out of one family’s desire to inspire, is the joyous food manifesto we didn’t know we needed.”

—ANDREW ZIMMERN, eater of the bizarre and the beautiful

“If you’re like me, and the word ‘leftovers’ doesn’t make you jump up and down, you need this book. Tiffani makes yesterday’s meals and kitchen scraps exciting again, with a thrilling amount of flavor, creativity, and fun. If my mother had had this book I would have complained 82 percent less.”

—PHIL ROSENTHAL, host and author of *Somebody Feed Phil*

“Tiffani is giving me all the retro feels with her latest cookbook, *Here We Go Again*. Recipes like her Cornbread Skillet Sloppy Joes and Old-School Ham Salad, I feel like I stepped back into my childhood. And can we talk about her Hurricane Granitas??? OH MY! Those will be on repeat by the pool all summer long. Cheers to another beautiful book that I know my family and I will be cooking from all year long.”

—SARAH MICHELLE GELLAR, slayer of many things

Here We Go Again

Here We Go Again

Recipes & Inspiration to Level Up Your Leftovers

TIFFANI THIESSEN

with Rachel Holtzman

NEW YORK NASHVILLE

Worthy Books
Hachette Book Group
1290 Avenue of the Americas, New York, NY 10104
WorthyPublishing.com
twitter.com/Worthy

First Edition: September 2023

Worthy is a division of Hachette Book Group, Inc. The Worthy name and logo are trademarks of Hachette Book Group, Inc.

The publisher is not responsible for websites (or their content) that are not owned by the publisher.

The Hachette Speakers Bureau provides a wide range of authors for speaking events. To find out more, go to www.hachettespeakersbureau.com or call (866) 376-6591.

Photographs by Rebecca Sanabria

Print book interior design by Laura Palese

Library of Congress Cataloging-in-Publication Data

Names: Thiessen, Tiffani, 1974- author. | Holtzman, Rachel, author.
Title: Here we go again : recipes and inspiration to level up your leftovers / Tiffani Thiessen with Rachel Holtzman.
Description: First edition. | New York, NY : Worthy Books, [2023] | Includes index.
Identifiers: LCCN 2022053120 | ISBN 9781546002765 (hardcover) | ISBN 9781546002772 (ebook)
Subjects: LCSH: Cooking (Leftovers) | LCGFT: Cookbooks.
Classification: LCC TX652 .T43 2023 | DDC 641.5/52--dc23/eng/20221121
LC record available at https://lccn.loc.gov/2022053120

ISBNs: 9781546002765 (hardcover), 9781546002772 (ebook)

Printed in China

RRD-SC

10 9 8 7 6 5 4 3 2 1

SONOMA MOUNTAIN

THIS BOOK IS DEDICATED TO

my mom,

who showed me the magic of leftovers.

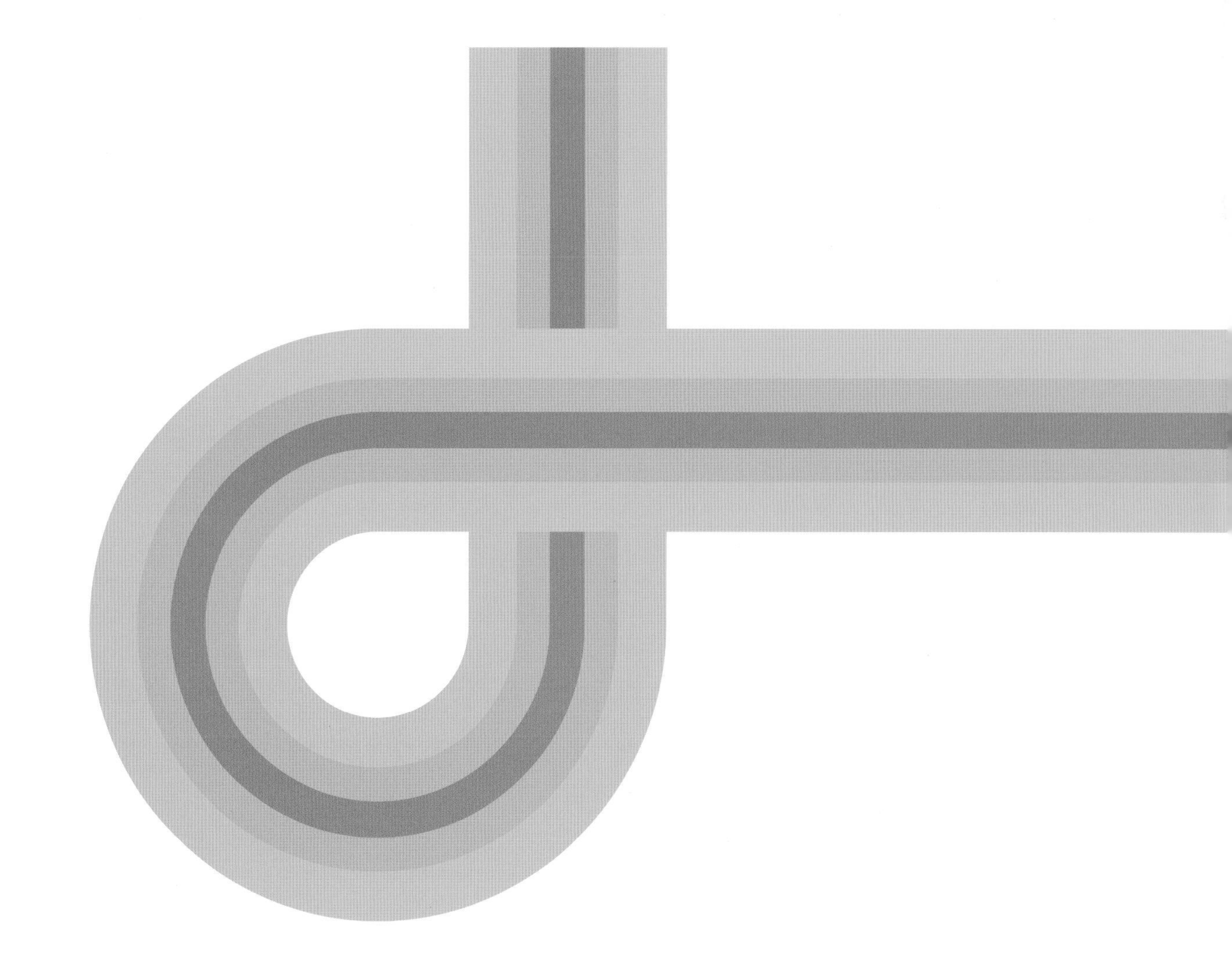

Contents

INTRODUCTION xvii

Baked French Toast with Jammy Whip **2**

Roasted Squash Bread Salad with Bacon-Dripping Vinaigrette **6**

Kale Caesar with Everything Croutons **9**

Cheddar & Sage Bread Pudding **12**

Greek to Me, New to You Pita Salad Bowls **14**

Pizza for Breakfast Sandwiches **19**

Bagel French Onion Soup **23**

Saucy Swedish Meatballs **24**

Lemony Breaded Pork Chops **28**

Cornbread Skillet Sloppy Joes **32**

MAKE IT FROM STARCH:
Pasta, Beans, Rice, & Potatoes
35

Buffalo Chicken Bean Dip **36**

Chicken Bone Soup with Rice **39**

Yesterday's Crispy Rice Cakes **40**

Mashed Potato Dumpling Soup **42**

Ciao, Arancini **47**

Clear-Out-the-Fridge Pasta Salad with Charred Tomato Dressing **48**

Spaghetti Pie, Oh My! **51**

Mimi's Chicken & Rice Casserole **53**

Mean Bean Burgers with Saffron Yogurt Sauce **54**

Fish & Tot Sandwiches **58**

Lemon Polenta Flapjacks **61**

Chocolate Spud Cake **64**

Tuna Salad Cakes with Tartar Sauce **70**

Throwback Pickled Shrimp Canapés **72**

Hot (Damn) Seafood Dip with Crackers **75**

Sausage, Beans, 'n' Greens **76**

Hamburger Junior VP **80**

Something-Borrowed Bourguignon **82**

Grilled Pulled Pork Burritos **86**

Waldorf Chicken Salad Lettuce Cups **91**

Surf & Turf Tacos **92**

The Produce Bin 97

No-Frills Frittata **98**

Eat Your Veg Muffins with Carrot-Oat Crumble **101**

Veggie Ramen Salad **104**

Savory Quinoa Porridge with Mushrooms **109**

Where's the Beet Patty Melts **110**

All-the-Veggies Shakshuka **114**

Any-Season Savory Tart **118**

(I'm So) Stuffed Shells **121**

Creamy Broccoli Soup with Cheddar "Crackers" **122**

Butternut Squash Quesadillas **124**

Rescue-Those-Berries Preserves **128**

Aunt Jenny's Sweet Potato Cake Roll **131**

Some Cheese Bits 135

Marinated Stuffed Olives **136**

All-the-Cheeses Spread & Fondue **138**

Cheese Drawer Soufflés **143**

Mixed-Mushroom Quiche **144**

Blue Cheese Buttah **146**

Cheesy Grits with Herbed Browned Butter **151**

Parmesan Cream Scalloped Potatoes **152**

Deluxe Grilled Cheese Sandwiches with Onion Jam **155**

Stuffed Zucchini "Subs" **156**

Parmesan Rind Cacio e Pepe **158**

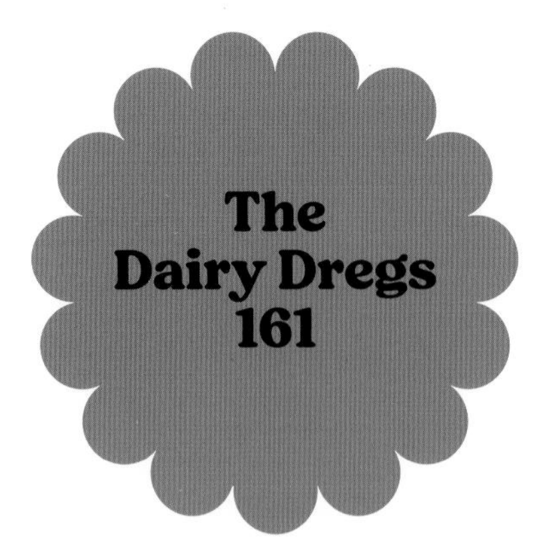

The Dairy Dregs 161

Cotton Candy Smoothies **162**

Retro Ambrosia Salad **165**

Smoked Salmon Omelet for One **166**

Dress-It-Up Dressings **168**

Buttermilk Horseradish Mashed Potatoes **173**

Chicken alla Vodka with Anchovy Breadcrumbs **174**

The Pink Lady **177**

Berry-Glazed Sour Cream Doughnuts **180**

Baby Baked Alaskas **185**

Bottom of the Bag, Box, & Bottle 187

Who Left the Chip Bag Open? Chilaquiles **188**

Bottom of the Pot Mocha Iced Latte **193**

Pretzel-Crumb Cheese Ball **194**

Cheese Cracker-Fried Chicken Sandwiches **198**

Nut-Crusted Fish **203**

Coffee-Glazed Pork Ribs **204**

Pickle-Brined Sauerbraten **208**

Cereal Milk Ice Pops **213**

Garbage Pound Cake **214**

The Last Pour **217**

Hurricane Granitas **221**

Squeaky Clean Martinis **222**

THE LEFTOVER OLYMPICS: Holidays 225

Champagne Crepes (Cheers!) **226**

Corned Beef Egg Rolls **229**

Old-School Ham Salad **232**

Pull-Apart Pigs in a Quilt **235**

Trick-or-Treat Fudge **236**

Thanksgiving Shepherd's Pie **241**

Latke Breakfast Hash with Greens **242**

Cranberry Sauce Cocktail **245**

Cheese Board Pinwheels **246**

Pot Roast & Potato Pizza **248**

Peppermint Hot Chocolate Cookies **252**

ACKNOWLEDGMENTS 255 • **INDEX 256** • **ABOUT THE AUTHOR 264**

California

Introduction

When I set out to write my first book, *Pull Up a Chair*, my goal was to get people to come back to the kitchen. I wanted to give readers a reason to hit the pause button and take a little bit of time to put something homemade on the table. Believe me, I'm no stranger to carrot sticks, store-bought hummus, and a rotisserie chicken for dinner—sometimes survival is the name of the game!—but I also grew up in a home where family mealtime was not something you messed with. My father worked two jobs so my mom could stay home with us kids—a full-time job in and of itself—so you better believe that when he walked in the door, my two brothers and I had our butts in seats at the dinner table. So to me, dinnertime has always been sacred.

When it came time to think about what I wanted to tackle in my next book, I again thought about how important family mealtime is, and yet how unrealistic it is to expect that any of us can make every dinner as fresh and exciting as the last. Toss in the fact that sometimes it can feel like we're line cooks in our own kitchens, cranking out multiple meals a day, seven days a week, and, well, I'm willing to bet that you're *way* over having to reinvent your menu like you're the executive chef of a fancy farm-to-table restaurant. So once again, I went back to my roots. You know what my mom's secret weapon was? Leftovers.

You know what my mom's secret weapon was? Leftovers.

YUP—leftovers. That most underrated workhorse of the kitchen! My mom was a big-batch cook, so there was *always* something from meals throughout the week that we'd be served again, oftentimes with a remix. You'd be amazed at how she could whip up something absolutely ingenious from the tasty bits, scraps, and extra ingredients lying around. As a result, I never dreaded leftovers night—in fact, I don't even think I could tell you which night it was. Most of the time we had no *idea* we were eating Monday's pasta in Wednesday's casserole or Tuesday's taco filling in Thursday's shepherd's pie. That's because my mom knew how to keep it feeling new by using leftovers as the foundation of a dish but then reaching for a different preparation or pairing them with fresh ingredients. It's been my goal in my own family to bring the same creative spark to our leftovers night too.

Let's face it, leftovers are a reality for those of us making weeknight suppers. And not only can eating the same thing twice or even three times a week become a snooze, but sometimes even that plan can be foiled if some people, who shall go nameless (*cough* the kids *cough*), weren't big fans the first time around. But leftovers can be so much more than the sum of their parts. Yesterday's dinner, last week's baking experiment, snack drawer remnants, and cheese drawer bits and bobs are all an opportunity to create something new and delicious. And don't even get me started on the holidays—they're a leftovers gold mine!

Leftovers are a reality for those of us making weeknight suppers.

Here We Go Again is dedicated to the recipes your leftovers deserve, whether they're the classics in your rotation, the dishes that maybe didn't hit the spot the first time around, or those last-ditch meal efforts you throw at your kids, only to have half of them still left in the pot. They're also perfect for ingredients that would otherwise be trash-bound—those carrots threatening to go soft, the bunches of kale from the overenthusiastic farmers market haul, that half loaf of bread getting harder by the day, the nubbins of cheese that don't seem good for anything other than late-night snacking. Or the dreaded remnants of sour cream or buttermilk inevitably left in the back of the fridge from when you made something else with it. I refuse to let all that dairy goodness go to waste! Or maybe it's the chicken breasts or steaks you stocked up on when they were on sale and are now sitting in your freezer, waiting for an invitation to be used. Or all the food staring back at you from your fridge after a big celebratory meal (and that you worked way too hard on to throw away!).

These are the dishes that we need right now—and in so many ways. We need to get food on the table, every day. We need to use the food that we have because we don't always know when we'll get to the store or how far we need to make our budget stretch. We need to be thinking about how we can get more mileage out of the food we have—and not be throwing so much away (something that we talk about all the

time in our house because creating less food waste is one simple way we can all pitch in to help the planet). And above all else, we need to take care of ourselves and our families with food that tastes good. Here you'll find my favorite easy-to-follow, family-approved recipes using inexpensive ingredients that you can find in your local grocery store, with plenty of suggested substitutions and variations to make these recipes as flexible and suited to the contents of your fridge and pantry as possible.

There will be some very familiar faces flavor-wise (Baked French Toast with Jammy Whip, Parmesan Rind Cacio e Pepe, Cornbread Skillet Sloppy Joes); along with plenty of Tex-Mex, thanks to my husband Brady's influence (Who Left the Chip Bag Open? Chilaquiles, Grilled Pulled Pork Burritos, Surf and Turf Tacos); and some fun, unexpected twists (Pizza for Breakfast Sandwiches, Chocolate Spud Cake, Cheese Cracker-Fried Chicken Sandwiches—that's right, all those pesky cheese cracker crumbs make a genius crispy coating for fried chicken). Oh, and while I'm at it, I'm going to throw in a fun retro '70s vibe. It's not only one of my favorite vibes as a child of the 1970s, but it also calls to mind some of my favorite comfort food dishes—can you say hot seafood dip, anything in a pinwheel, and macaroni salad? These throwback classics are the perfect, fun canvases for giving new life to leftovers—after all, what's old is new again!

Whether it's my insanely tempting (and addicting) Spaghetti Pie, Oh My!, my Something-Borrowed Bourguignon that uses up last night's roast plus the vegetables in your crisper, my delectable Buttermilk Horseradish Mashed Potatoes recipe that gets its secret-ingredient creamy tanginess from the last pour of buttermilk left in the carton (or cream cheese or heavy cream), or the choose-your-favorite-cereal-studded Cereal Milk Ice Pops that my kids beg for all summer, these are recipes that truly bring the wow factor while using simple ingredients that you probably have in your kitchen. Don't let them go bad—put them to work! Or really, let them work for you. With just the right twist—and a sense of play—these dishes are guaranteed to be whole-family pleasers. That's what this book is all about: making the most of what your refrigerator and pantry have to offer, celebrating the joy of delicious food, and making your time around the table special (even if it's technically your dinner's second time around). But that will be our little secret...

I can't wait to see what you cook up!

Tiffani

These throwback classics are the perfect, fun canvases for giving new life to leftovers.

BUST THE Crust

Bread

I don't think there's anything as tragic as a delicious loaf of bread that seems perfectly fresh at the store one day...and like a lump of concrete the next. Even if you're lucky enough to get a couple of slices out of it, it still feels like a waste. Luckily, there's no shortage of second chances for that loaf, from slathering it in olive oil and toasting it until golden and crisp for a panzanella (a fancy name for "bread salad") or croutons, to bathing it in an egg mixture for baked French toast or a savory bread pudding, to grinding it up into breadcrumbs. And that's not even including what's possible for other bread-box regulars like bagels, pitas, and hamburger and hot dog buns—all of which are way too good to toss once they've passed peak freshness. The best part about these recipes is that stale, dried-out bread is *preferable*—the better to soak up all that flavor! If you ask me, it's the perfect excuse to bring home even more bread.

Baked French Toast

with Jammy Whip

Brunch is a big deal in my house. At least once a weekend we dedicate a lazy morning to getting out of bed a little more slowly than usual, then camping out in the kitchen while we all make breakfast together. It's such a nice change of pace from running around like maniacs while we load up backpacks and throw cereal into bowls and toast into the toaster. But while there's more time to pull together classic hot-breakfast staples like pancakes and waffles, I'm a really big fan of this baked French toast because it can be prepped the night before, be left to soak overnight, then get popped into the oven in the morning—a major bonus if you have company joining you. When it's topped with whipped cream swirled with preserves, it's like tucking into the most delicious breakfast-approved bread pudding.

Half-and-half

Heavy cream

French Toast

Unsalted butter, for greasing

1¼ cups half-and-half

5 large eggs

½ cup maple syrup

⅓ cup lightly packed light brown sugar

Zest of 1 orange or lemon

1 teaspoon ground cinnamon

1 teaspoon pure vanilla bean paste or extract

¼ teaspoon kosher salt

5 slices brioche bread (6 ounces), preferably stale, cut into 1-inch cubes (see Note)

Jammy Whip

½ cup heavy cream

1 tablespoon liquid from Rescue-Those-Berries Preserves (page 128) or jam of your choice, plus more for serving

Note

Brioche or challah is ideal, but this recipe would also work with other breads, including sliced white bread. Also, if you choose to make the French toast ahead and bake it directly from the fridge, you may need to increase the bake time by 5 to 10 minutes.

- **Make the French toast:** Preheat the oven to 350°F. Lightly grease an 8 x 8-inch baking dish with butter and set aside.
- In a medium bowl, whisk together the half-and-half, eggs, maple syrup, brown sugar, orange zest, cinnamon, vanilla bean paste, and salt. Gently fold in the bread cubes until they're evenly coated. Pour the mixture into the prepared dish and let the bread soak for 15 minutes to absorb most of the liquid, or cover the bowl with plastic wrap and refrigerate overnight.
- Bake for 45 minutes, or until the custard is completely set and a knife or skewer inserted into the center comes out clean. Let the French toast rest for 10 to 15 minutes.
- **Meanwhile, make the jammy whip:** In the bowl of a stand mixer fitted with the whisk attachment or in a medium bowl with a hand blender or whisk, whip together the heavy cream with the preserve liquid or jam until soft peaks form.
- Serve the French toast with a dollop of the whipped cream and more preserves, if desired.

Jam

Baked French Toast with Jammy Whip
PAGE 2

joy
Jam

Roasted Squash Bread Salad

with Bacon-Dripping Vinaigrette

Panzanella is a traditional Tuscan dish that is quite literally bread salad. It is a flavorful way to give stale bread new life because something magical happens when big cubes of it are doused in olive oil, toasted until golden brown, and tossed with vinaigrette: The outside gets caramelized and crispy while the inside, which has soaked up all that good oil and vinegar like a sponge, gets back some of its original soft suppleness. Tossed together with sweet roasted squash and a smoky vinaigrette made with bacon drippings (another great second-time-around hack!), this dish is the perfect one-bowl lunch or dinner.

Bacon drippings

Bitter greens like radicchio and escarole

Kale or other hearty greens

Creamy cheese such as burrata, mozzarella, goat, or Brie

Bacon-Dripping Vinaigrette

½ cup aged balsamic vinegar

2 tablespoons fresh lemon juice (about 1 lemon)

2 tablespoons Dijon mustard

1 teaspoon kosher salt

¼ teaspoon freshly ground black pepper, plus more to taste

½ cup rendered bacon fat, warmed (see Note)

Bread Salad

1 pound squash, such as kabocha, butternut, or acorn, peeled and cut into ¼-inch-thick wedges (about 3 cups)

¼ cup plus 2 tablespoons extra-virgin olive oil

¾ teaspoon kosher salt

1 large red onion, thinly sliced (about 1 cup)

6 slices day-old bread, ideally sourdough, cut into 1-inch cubes (about 6 cups)

2 garlic cloves, minced

½ small head escarole, cut into ½-inch dice (about 3 cups)

¼ head radicchio, cored and cut into ¼-inch dice (about 1 cup)

4 leaves kale or other hearty green, stems removed and leaves cut into ¼-inch strips (about 2 cups)

1 yellow peach, nectarine, or apple, pitted and cut into ¼-inch-thick wedges (about 1 cup)

6 ounces creamy cheese such as burrata, mozzarella, goat, or Brie, torn or crumbled (about 1 heaping cup)

Freshly ground black pepper

- **Make the vinaigrette:** In a medium bowl, whisk together the balsamic vinegar, lemon juice, mustard, salt, and pepper. Slowly stream in the bacon fat, whisking, until the dressing is emulsified. Season with more black pepper to taste. Use immediately or store in an airtight container in the refrigerator for up to 5 days. If refrigerating, warm the dressing over very low heat and whisk to combine before using.

- **Make the bread salad:** Preheat the oven to 400°F.

CONTINUES

balance

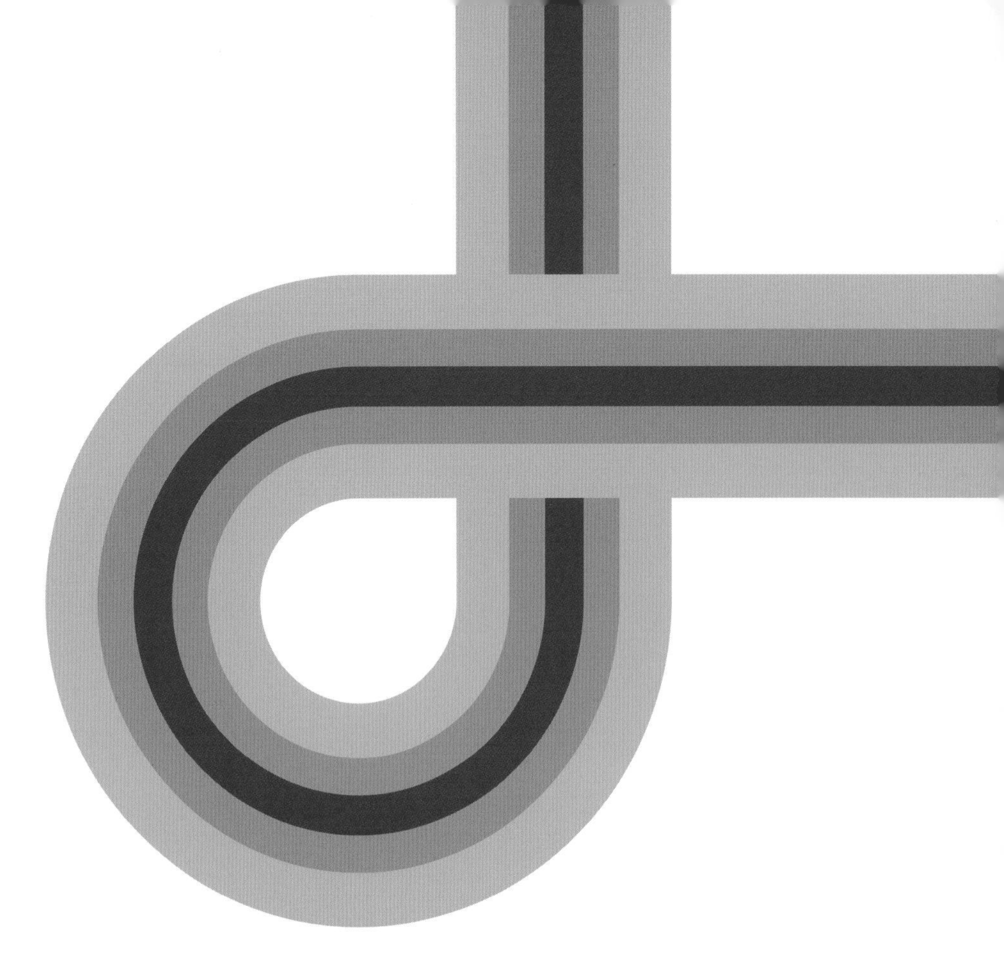

Note

Anytime I cook bacon, I wait for the grease to cool, then pour it into a glass jar that I keep in my fridge. (Shout-out to my mom, who always kept a can's worth on the kitchen counter.) It lasts for a few months in the refrigerator and pretty much forever in the freezer and can be used in place of olive oil, especially when sautéing vegetables or making vinaigrettes. If you don't have rendered bacon fat on hand to make this dressing, you can use extra-virgin olive oil instead. If you have some rendered bacon fat but not a full ½ cup, use what you have and swap in olive oil for the rest.

● In a medium bowl, toss the squash with 1 tablespoon of the olive oil and ¼ teaspoon of the salt. Spread the squash evenly over half of a baking sheet. In the same medium bowl, toss the red onion with 1 tablespoon of the olive oil and ¼ teaspoon of the salt and spread the onions evenly over the other half of the baking sheet.

● Roast the squash and onions for 20 minutes, or until the onions have softened and are just beginning to caramelize at the edges and the squash is deep golden brown on the bottom. Transfer the onions to a plate. Flip the squash over and roast for an additional 6 minutes, or until it is golden brown on the other side. Set aside to cool and leave the oven on.

● In a medium bowl, toss the bread cubes with the remaining ¼ cup olive oil, the remaining ¼ teaspoon salt, and the garlic, making sure they are evenly coated. Spread the mixture over a second baking sheet and bake for 10 to 12 minutes, until the bread is golden brown at the edges. Let cool slightly, about 5 minutes, then toss the bread with ¼ cup of the dressing to coat. Set aside.

● In a large bowl, combine the escarole, radicchio, kale, and peach. Toss the salad with ¼ cup of the dressing and fold in the bread cubes. Transfer the bread salad to a serving bowl and tear the burrata over the top. Serve with another drizzle of the dressing and a few cracks of freshly ground black pepper.

Kale Caesar

with Everything Croutons

Making croutons out of less-than-fresh bread is Leftovers 101. But the level-up here is tossing them with "everything" seasoning, which gives any salad even more flavorful dimension. I love pairing these croutons with a classic kale Caesar for a dish that tastes way more sophisticated and elaborate than the simple preparation it is.

Egg yolks

Everything Croutons

1 ciabatta or dinner roll, or other bread (sourdough, French, Texas toast), cut into ½-inch cubes (about 2½ cups)

3 tablespoons extra-virgin olive oil

3 tablespoons everything bagel seasoning (see Notes on page 10)

Caesar Dressing

2 slices smoked salmon (about 1 ounce)

2 teaspoons brined capers, drained

1 large garlic clove, minced

2 large egg yolks

2 tablespoons fresh lemon juice (about 1 lemon)

1 teaspoon Dijon mustard

½ teaspoon kosher salt

¼ teaspoon freshly ground black pepper

¼ cup plus 2 tablespoons vegetable oil

2 tablespoons grated Parmesan cheese

To Assemble

2 bunches Tuscan kale (about 20 leaves), stems removed

1 large red onion, thinly sliced (about 1 cup)

¼ cup brined capers, drained

6 slices smoked salmon (about 3 ounces; see Notes on page 10)

Freshly grated Parmesan cheese, for serving

- **Make the croutons:** Preheat the oven to 400°F.

- In a medium bowl, toss the cubed bread with the olive oil and seasoning mix to evenly coat. Spread the cubes over a baking sheet in an even layer. Use a rubber spatula to scrape every bit of the seasoning mixture out of the bowl and onto the bread. Bake for 12 to 14 minutes, tossing the croutons halfway through, until the croutons are crispy and a deep golden brown all over. Set aside.

- **Make the dressing:** Place the smoked salmon, capers, and garlic on a cutting board. Chop until the mixture becomes a fine paste. Set aside.

- In a medium bowl, whisk together the egg yolks, lemon juice, and mustard until smooth. Whisk in the smoked salmon mixture along with the salt and pepper to combine. While continuing to whisk, slowly stream in the oil until the dressing is emulsified. Stir in the grated Parmesan.

- **Assemble the salad:** In a large bowl, toss together the kale, red onion, capers, and everything croutons. Add enough dressing to lightly coat the salad and toss to evenly distribute. Transfer the salad to a serving platter or bowl, top with smoked salmon slices, and drizzle with more dressing to taste. Serve with the Parmesan.

Notes

This is a great make-ahead dish. You can make the croutons ahead of time and store them in a tightly sealed container at room temperature for up to 3 days. You can also make the dressing and store it in an airtight container in the refrigerator for up to 3 days.

For the everything seasoning, you can find premade mixes in most grocery stores, or you can make your own by combining poppy seeds, sesame seeds, minced dried garlic, minced dried onion, and flaked sea salt.

If you don't love smoked salmon or don't have it on hand, smoked whitefish would work well here. You could also leave the smoked salmon out of the dressing and top the salad with any grilled protein such as chicken.

Kale Caesar with Everything Croutons
PAGE 9

Cheddar & Sage Bread Pudding

I'm all for a dish that can be thrown together in advance, then baked and served fresh and hot out of the oven. I'm also majorly all for a dish that takes custardy bread pudding and gives it a cheesy, savory spin with plenty of fresh sage. And, as with all the other recipes in this chapter, it's ideal if you're using bread that's on the dried-out side—which is a major plus in the leftovers department. I'll serve this for a decadent brunch, or for lunch or dinner alongside a simple, fresh salad.

Fresh sage

Shredded cheese

Whole milk

Note

To make this the night before, cover the bread pudding with plastic wrap once you've assembled all the ingredients in the baking dish and refrigerate. Let the bread pudding sit at room temperature for 30 minutes before baking.

4 heaping cups day-old baguette, sourdough, French bread, or ciabatta, torn into 1-inch pieces

6 tablespoons unsalted butter, cut into 1-inch cubes

2 tablespoons extra-virgin olive oil

1 shallot, thinly sliced (about ¼ cup)

4 garlic cloves, smashed

3 large sprigs fresh sage

3 (1-inch) strips lemon peel

2 teaspoons kosher salt

½ teaspoon smoked paprika

4 large eggs

2 cups whole milk

1½ cups shredded cheese (I like extra-sharp cheddar here)

¼ teaspoon freshly ground black pepper

10 cherry tomatoes

- Preheat the oven to 350°F.
- Spread the bread evenly over a baking sheet and set aside.
- In an 8 x 8-inch baking dish, combine the butter, olive oil, shallot, garlic, sage, lemon peel, 1 teaspoon of the salt, and the paprika. Place both the baking sheet with the torn bread and the baking dish in the oven for 20 minutes, or until the bread is lightly toasted and the shallot and garlic have softened. Keep the oven on.
- Remove the lemon peel and discard. Remove the sage sprigs and set aside. Transfer the butter mixture to a medium bowl. (Don't clean out the baking dish! Everything will ultimately go back in.) Add the bread and toss to coat with the butter mixture. Transfer everything back to the baking dish.
- In the same medium bowl, whisk together the eggs, milk, 1 cup of the shredded cheese, the remaining 1 teaspoon salt, and the black pepper. Pour the custard mixture evenly over the bread and top with the remaining ½ cup shredded cheese. Tear the leaves of the reserved sage and scatter them over the top of the cheddar. Then nestle the cherry tomatoes evenly over the mixture.
- Bake for 30 minutes, or until the cheese is melted and beginning to crisp on the edges, the tomatoes are soft and just beginning to burst, and a knife or skewer inserted into the center comes out clean. Serve immediately.

Greek to Me, New to You Pita Salad Bowls

Pita tends to have two modes: fluffy, pillowy, and delightful...and cardboard. Luckily, you don't have to toss them when they're no longer ideal for stuffing as sandwiches. Instead, you can slather them in olive oil, sesame seeds, and oregano and bake them until they're toasty and golden. But the best part? You can mold them in the oven so they're shaped like bowls and then fill them with Greek salad for a fun play on the traditional dish. My kids love how they can tear off pieces of the pita, then scoop up all their favorite bits of cucumbers, tomatoes, olives, and Halloumi cheese. The bowls are on the smaller side, but the more you refill them with salad, the more flavorful the pita gets!

Fresh parsley

Red onion

Romaine hearts

Pita Bowls

1 tablespoon plus 1 teaspoon extra-virgin olive oil

2 tablespoons za'atar (see Notes)

2 pitas

Dressing

½ vine-ripened tomato, grated (about ¼ cup)

1 small garlic clove, minced

2 tablespoons finely chopped fresh parsley

1 tablespoon red wine vinegar

1 tablespoon honey

1 teaspoon Dijon mustard

¾ teaspoon kosher salt

½ teaspoon dried oregano leaves

¼ cup extra-virgin olive oil

Freshly ground black pepper

Greek Salad

2 large eggs

2 tablespoons extra-virgin olive oil

4 (½-inch-thick) slices Halloumi

1 romaine heart, chopped into 1-inch pieces (about 4 cups)

2 Persian cucumbers, quartered lengthwise and cut into ¼-inch pieces (about 2 cups)

1½ vine-ripened tomatoes, cut into ¼-inch dice (about 1 cup)

1 (15-ounce) can chickpeas, drained and rinsed

½ cup pitted Kalamata olives, halved lengthwise

½ small red onion, thinly sliced (about ½ cup)

- **Make the pita bowls:** Preheat the oven to 350°F.
- In a small bowl, whisk together the olive oil and za'atar. Set aside.
- Microwave the pitas for 20 seconds to soften and then cut in half. If your pita doesn't have a pocket, use a paring knife to gently cut a pocket into the pita, making sure not to cut a hole through the outer edge. Tear 4 pieces of aluminum foil about the size of half a baking sheet. Make a tightly packed half-moon shape with each of them, mimicking the shape of the inside of the pita, and gently insert them into the opening of each pita. You want the foil to hold the pita open at least 3 inches wide as it bakes.

● Brush the outside of each pita with the olive oil mixture. Bake for 20 minutes, or until the pita is set and the outside is golden brown. When cool enough to handle, gently remove the foil.

● **While the pita bakes, make the salad dressing and the salad:** In a small bowl, combine the tomato, garlic, parsley, vinegar, honey, mustard, salt, and oregano. Whisk to combine. Continue whisking as you slowly stream in the olive oil and the dressing is emulsified. Season with black pepper to taste. Use immediately, or store in an airtight container in the refrigerator for up to 1 week.

● Fill a small bowl with ice water and set aside. In a small saucepan, add the eggs and cover with cold water. Bring to a boil over medium-high heat, then remove the pan from the heat and let stand for 4 minutes for a soft-boiled egg and up to 10 minutes for a hard-boiled egg. Transfer the eggs to the ice bath to cool completely before peeling and slicing in half lengthwise.

● Heat the olive oil in a small nonstick sauté pan over medium heat. Swirl the pan so it is evenly coated with the oil and add the Halloumi slices. Cook until deeply golden brown on each side, about 3 minutes per side. Transfer the cheese to a cutting board. When cool enough to handle, slice the cheese into ¼-inch cubes.

● In a large bowl, combine the Halloumi, romaine, cucumbers, tomatoes, chickpeas, olives, and red onion. Toss with the salad dressing and divide among the cooled pita bowls. Top each bowl with half an egg and serve. You can continue to refill your pita bowls with more salad—the more salad you add, the more flavorful the pita becomes!

Notes

This recipe calls for za'atar, an earthy Mediterranean/Middle Eastern spice blend. I personally love keeping a container in my pantry and using it to add dimension and flavor to things like grilled bread, toasted pitas, roasted chicken, steak, potatoes, and hummus. But if you'd prefer, you could also substitute 1 tablespoon plus 1 teaspoon white sesame seeds, 2 teaspoons dried oregano leaves, and 1 teaspoon kosher salt. If using za'atar, check to see if your blend includes salt. If not, add 1 teaspoon kosher salt when blending with the olive oil.

And while I love making this recipe with Greek flavors, you can customize it any way you want: Brush the outside with any dried herbs and spices you have and fill with your favorite salads or dips.

Greek to Me, New to You
Pita Salad Bowls
PAGE 14

Pizza for Breakfast Sandwiches

Pizza is one of my favorite easy dinners to make because it means one of two things: Either I've thrown together a batch of my easy homemade dough from *Pull Up a Chair* and we all get to choose our toppings, or I've put in a call to our neighborhood pizzeria and ordered an extra-large cheese pie. Either way, we all win. It also means that there's usually a few slices of leftovers hanging out in our fridge. So I've come up with a way to turn them into the ultimate breakfast (which doesn't include me eating it cold from the fridge).

Whole-milk ricotta

Fresh basil

4 large slices of cold pizza (see Note)

1 cup grated Parmesan cheese

4 slices prosciutto (about 2 ounces)

¼ cup whole-milk ricotta

Zest of 1 lemon

Kosher salt and freshly ground black pepper

2 tablespoons extra-virgin olive oil

4 large eggs

Calabrian chili oil or red chili flakes

12 fresh basil leaves, torn

- Preheat the oven to 375°F. Line two baking sheets with parchment paper.

- Arrange the pizza slices on the prepared baking sheets so that there is plenty of room between the slices. Next, you're going to create what will become the top for each sandwich, the Parmesan cracker. Begin by sprinkling ¼ cup of the cheese along the longest edge of a pizza slice. Use your fingers to spread the cheese into a thin, even layer along the entire edge of the pizza and then continue spreading out the cheese until it forms a half-moon. (The edge of the pizza will be the base of the half-moon.) Repeat with the remaining slices of pizza and the remaining Parmesan. Lay the slices of prosciutto in a single layer in between the pizza slices and cheese so that they are directly on the baking sheet.

- Bake for 15 minutes, or until the Parmesan is melted and golden brown around the edges, the pizza is heated through, and the prosciutto is crispy. Let everything sit for 5 minutes so the Parmesan sets and crisps up even more.

- In a small bowl, whisk together the ricotta and lemon zest. Season with salt and pepper to taste and set aside.

CONTINUES

natural preserved lemon
SHRUBS
PLUM
MARINATED GARLIC
UNE FEMME
UNE FEMME
La Croix
La Croix
SQUEEZE

● Heat the olive oil in a medium nonstick sauté pan over medium-low heat. Crack an egg into a small bowl and then pour the egg into the pan. Repeat with the remaining eggs. Season each egg with a pinch of salt and cook until the whites have set, about 2 minutes. Drizzle each egg with chili oil (if using red chili flakes, wait to add them) and continue frying until the edges are browned and the yolk is cooked to medium, about another 2 minutes. Transfer the eggs to a plate.

● Carefully flip the pizza slices onto plates. It's okay if some of the frico cracks! Divide the ricotta evenly among the slices and spread it over the pizza. Add the torn basil over the top, followed by a fried egg. If you are using red chili flakes instead of chili oil, sprinkle them over the eggs. Finish with the crispy prosciutto and gently fold the Parmesan cracker over the pizza like you're closing a book. Serve immediately.

Note

I usually make this recipe using large triangular slices of pizza, but you can use any style and size of slice; you may need to adjust how much Parmesan you're using. Also, feel free to use pizza with any sort of toppings—you can customize your sandwich toppings to make sure it's a good match.

Bagel French Onion Soup

Harper is a bagel *freak*—that girl could eat a bagel for breakfast, lunch, and dinner and do it all over again the next day. (What can I say, she gets it from her mama!) I usually stash them in the freezer while they're still good and fresh after a day or two, but every once in a while, they end up getting tough and chewy on me. Sure, I could pop 'em into the toaster and call it a day, but I think it's a lot more fun to use them as an excuse to make this deliciously twisted version of French onion soup. It's got the same deeply flavored broth as a traditional version, but instead of French bread sitting under layers of melty Gruyère, that's where you'll find a perfectly toasty bagel.

Fresh thyme

Fresh parsley

Bourbon

Note

You can use just about any savory flavor of bagel for this recipe—plain, poppy seed, onion, sesame seed. Also, this recipe calls for stock, but if you don't have enough, you can make up the remaining amount in water.

2 tablespoons unsalted butter

2 tablespoons extra-virgin olive oil

2 large yellow onions, thinly sliced (about 4 cups)

6 sprigs fresh thyme

¼ cup bourbon

6 cups beef, chicken, or vegetable stock (see Note)

2 teaspoons kosher salt

½ teaspoon freshly ground black pepper

1 teaspoon sherry vinegar

2 bagels, preferably stale, halved (see Note)

2 cups grated Gruyère cheese

Roughly chopped fresh parsley, for serving

- Preheat the oven to broil. Line a large baking sheet with foil and set aside.

- In a medium saucepan over medium-low heat, add the butter with the olive oil and stir to coat the pan. Cook until the butter is melted, about 1 minute. Add the onions and stir to coat them in the butter and oil. Add the thyme and cook, stirring occasionally, until the onions are softened and begin to caramelize, about 16 minutes.

- Add the bourbon, using a wooden spoon to scrape up any brown bits from the bottom of the pan. Cook, stirring often, until the onions have caramelized to a deep golden brown, about another 6 minutes. Remove the thyme and discard. Stir in the stock, salt, and pepper. Bring the mixture to a simmer over medium-high heat and cook for 5 more minutes. Remove the pan from the heat and stir in the sherry vinegar.

- Divide the soup among four 16-ounce oven-safe bowls or ramekins. Score the outside of each bagel half with a serrated knife, making slits every ½ inch and being careful not to cut all the way through the bagel. Turn the bagel 45 degrees and then make cuts in the opposite direction to create a crosshatch pattern. You can skip this step, but it will ensure that a day-old bagel will soak up even more of the soup. It will also be easier to break apart as you eat it.

- Add ¼ cup of the cheese to each bowl. Top with a scored bagel half, flat side down, followed by another ¼ cup of cheese. Place the bowls on the prepared baking sheet and broil for 3 to 4 minutes, until the cheese is bubbly in the center, crispy around the edges, and deep golden brown all over. Sprinkle with parsley and serve.

Saucy Swedish Meatballs

One of the key ingredients of a great meatball is, that's right, bread. When soaked in milk, bread becomes the ultimate binder, while also keeping the meatballs from tasting densely "meaty." So until hot dog and hot dog bun manufacturers get on board with offering the same number of items in a package, this is a great way to repurpose your extra buns. Or hamburger buns. Or slices of white bread that aren't sandwich-caliber anymore. I'm also especially fond of this recipe because of my stroganoff-style twist, a creamy mushroom gravy. All you need to do is serve these with egg noodles or Buttermilk Horseradish Mashed Potatoes (page 173), and maybe a dollop of Rescue-Those-Berries Preserves (page 128), for an extra-Swedish touch.

Whole milk

Yellow onion

Fresh thyme

Vermouth

Heavy cream

Mashed potatoes

Meatballs

2 tablespoons vegetable oil

½ cup whole milk

2 large eggs

2 teaspoons kosher salt

½ teaspoon freshly ground black pepper

2 hamburger or hot dog buns (about 4 ounces), torn into small pieces

1 pound ground beef (I prefer 80/20, but 85/15 or 90/10 would work as well, just provide less fat/moisture)

½ large yellow onion, finely diced (about 1 cup)

6 garlic cloves, minced

Gravy

4 tablespoons unsalted butter

8 ounces cremini mushrooms (stems included), thinly sliced (about 2 cups)

6 sprigs fresh thyme

1 teaspoon ground allspice

½ teaspoon kosher salt, plus more to taste

½ teaspoon ground white pepper

¼ cup dry vermouth

2 tablespoons all-purpose flour

2 cups low-sodium beef stock

½ cup heavy cream

1 tablespoon Worcestershire sauce

Serve With

Prepared mashed potatoes (such as Buttermilk Horseradish Mashed Potatoes, page 173) or cooked egg noodles

Rescue-Those-Berries Preserves (page 128; optional)

Chopped fresh parsley

- **Make the meatballs:** Preheat the oven to 400°F. Line a rimmed baking sheet with foil and rub with the oil to coat. Set aside.

- In a large bowl, whisk together the milk, eggs, salt, and pepper. Add in the torn buns and use your hands to push the bread into the milk so it absorbs the liquid. Continue using your hands to mix in the beef, onion, and garlic until just combined. (The less you mix, the more tender your meatballs will be.)

● Divide the meat mixture into 20 golf ball–sized meatballs. Evenly arrange the meatballs on the prepared sheet and rotate them so they get coated on all sides with the oil. Bake for 25 minutes, or until the meatballs are cooked through and deeply golden brown. Let them rest while you make the gravy.

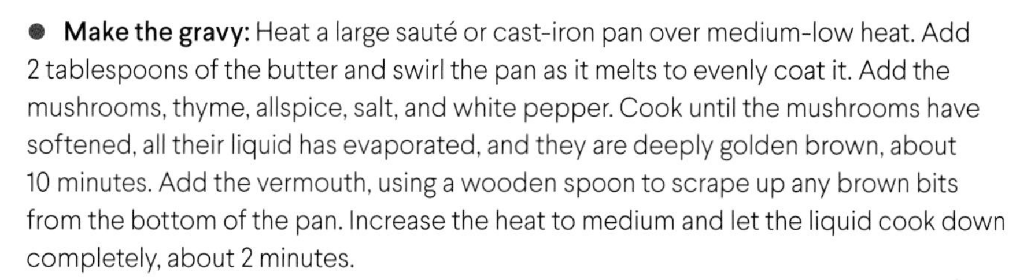

● **Make the gravy:** Heat a large sauté or cast-iron pan over medium-low heat. Add 2 tablespoons of the butter and swirl the pan as it melts to evenly coat it. Add the mushrooms, thyme, allspice, salt, and white pepper. Cook until the mushrooms have softened, all their liquid has evaporated, and they are deeply golden brown, about 10 minutes. Add the vermouth, using a wooden spoon to scrape up any brown bits from the bottom of the pan. Increase the heat to medium and let the liquid cook down completely, about 2 minutes.

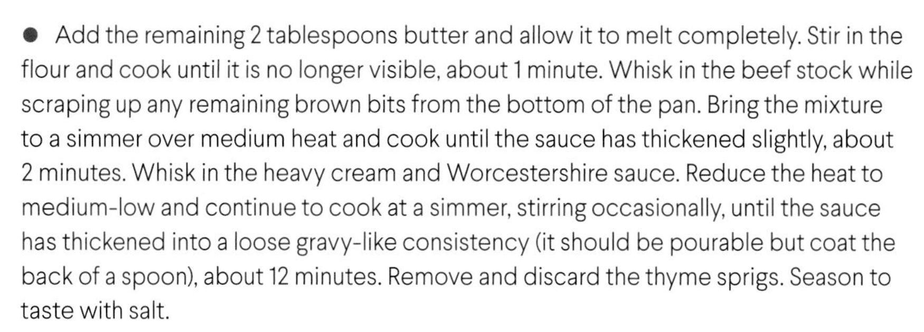

● Add the remaining 2 tablespoons butter and allow it to melt completely. Stir in the flour and cook until it is no longer visible, about 1 minute. Whisk in the beef stock while scraping up any remaining brown bits from the bottom of the pan. Bring the mixture to a simmer over medium heat and cook until the sauce has thickened slightly, about 2 minutes. Whisk in the heavy cream and Worcestershire sauce. Reduce the heat to medium-low and continue to cook at a simmer, stirring occasionally, until the sauce has thickened into a loose gravy-like consistency (it should be pourable but coat the back of a spoon), about 12 minutes. Remove and discard the thyme sprigs. Season to taste with salt.

● Reduce the heat to low and gently fold the meatballs into the sauce. Cook just until the meatballs are warmed through. Remove the pan from the heat.

● Serve the meatballs and gravy with mashed potatoes or egg noodles and preserves, if desired. Garnish with parsley.

Saucy Swedish Meatballs
PAGE 24

Lemony Breaded Pork Chops

One of the oldest cooking hacks in the book is to reincarnate dried-out bread as breadcrumbs. It's a win-win—you don't have to throw away that hard-as-rock heel of a loaf, and you end up with breadcrumbs that are way more flavorful than anything you can buy at the store. I love souping them up with Parmesan and lemon zest, which makes for an extra-delicious coating for fried pork chops. Serve this with a simple arugula salad or roasted vegetables and call it a day.

4 cups French loaf, ciabatta, or sourdough, cut or torn into small pieces, or 2 cups store-bought panko or other breadcrumbs

4 (1-inch-thick) boneless pork chops (about 2 pounds)

⅓ cup grated Parmesan cheese

Zest of 2 lemons (about 1 tablespoon)

2 teaspoons dried oregano leaves

1 teaspoon dry mustard powder

1 teaspoon onion powder

1 teaspoon garlic powder

1½ teaspoons kosher salt, plus more to taste

½ teaspoon freshly ground black pepper

½ cup all-purpose flour

2 large eggs

Vegetable oil, for frying

Lemon wedges, for serving

- Preheat the oven to 300°F.

- In the bowl of a food processor, process half of the bread until it is finely ground (about the texture of panko, if not finer). Transfer the breadcrumbs to a rimmed baking sheet and repeat with the remaining bread. Spread all the breadcrumbs in an even layer on the baking sheet and bake for 25 minutes, or until the breadcrumbs are lightly golden brown and completely dry, like the texture of crackers. Let cool completely, at least 20 minutes.

- Sandwich a pork chop between two layers of parchment paper or plastic wrap. Using a meat mallet, rolling pin, or the bottom of a skillet, pound the pork chop to ¼-inch thickness, being careful not to tear the meat and to keep the thickness even. Repeat with the remaining pork chops and set aside.

- In a medium bowl, combine the breadcrumbs with the Parmesan, lemon zest, oregano, mustard powder, onion powder, garlic powder, salt, and pepper. Use your hands to combine the mixture by pressing the breadcrumbs between your fingers to break up the lemon zest and ensure that it is evenly combined with the breadcrumbs. Set aside.

CONTINUES

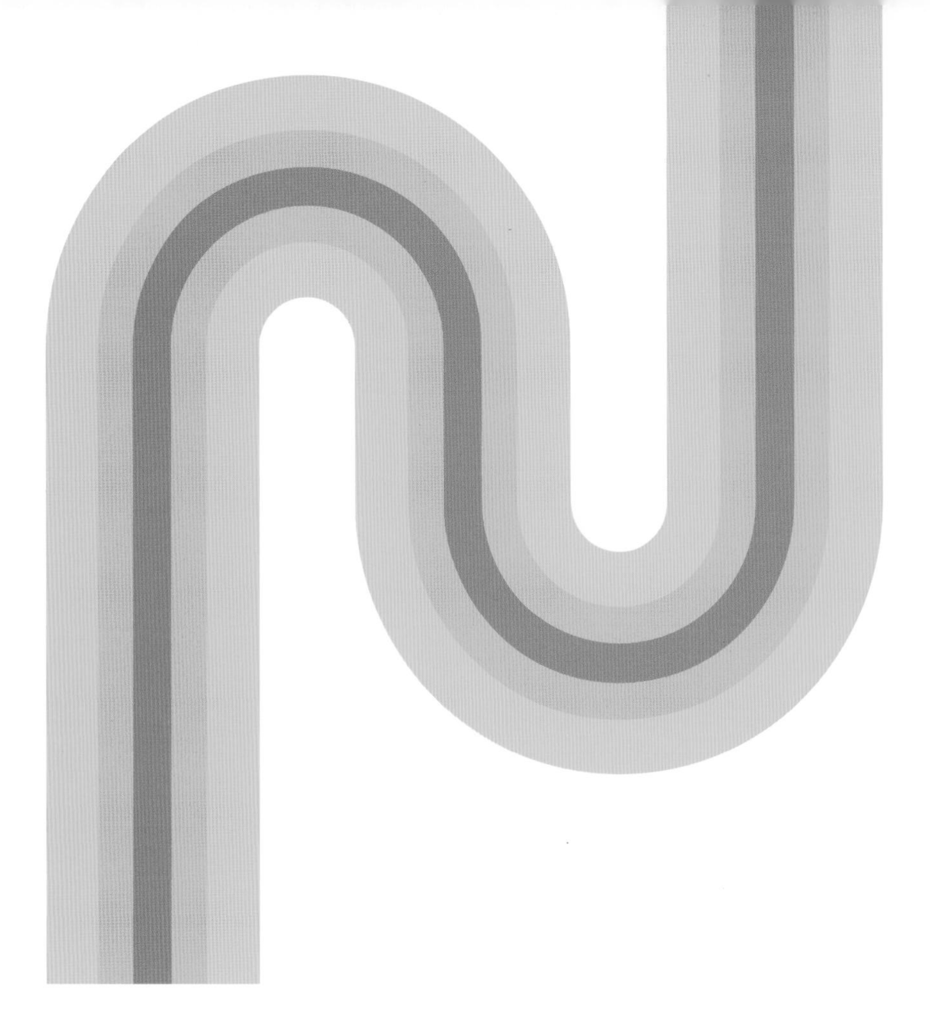

Note

While you're already making breadcrumbs, I highly recommend doubling the recipe and freezing half of the seasoned crumbs for another use. Store them in a zip-top bag (be sure to squeeze out any excess air!) for up to 3 months. There's also nothing wrong with using store-bought panko or other breadcrumbs, especially because they're getting so nicely seasoned.

- Add the flour to a shallow dish. In a second dish, whisk together the eggs. Dredge the pork chops in the flour, shaking off any excess. Next, coat the chops with the egg, allowing excess egg to drip off. Finally, coat each side of the pork chop with the breadcrumb mixture, using your hands to press the mixture into the chops so they are evenly covered.

- Line a large tray with paper towels and set aside.

- In a large sauté pan over medium heat, add enough oil to come ½ inch up the sides of the pan. Heat the oil until it shimmers. (If you have a thermometer, the oil should register at about 350°F.) Working in batches so as not to overcrowd the pan, add the pork chops and cook until the breadcrumbs are golden brown, 2 to 3 minutes. Flip and repeat on the other side. Transfer the cooked pork chops to the paper towel–lined tray and immediately season with salt. Make sure the oil in the pan has come back to temperature before repeating this process with the remaining pork chops. Serve with lemon wedges.

Cornbread Skillet Sloppy Joes

If you're like me, every once in a while you get a hankering for sweet-savory cornbread (hello, Skillet Cornbread, from *Pull Up a Chair*). Also if you're like me, you don't make your way through the whole pan before it starts to dry out. This recipe is the best of both worlds: You can scratch the itch for cornbread while also putting out a modernized version of this old-school fan favorite. Who doesn't remember (and love!) Sloppy Joes?! For this recipe, I've swapped out the buns for a skillet full of the signature saucy, tangy, meaty filling that gets baked with a cheesy do-over cornbread topping. Honestly, it's so good that you may find yourself buying cornbread just to make this recipe—and that's okay!

Tomato paste

Tomato sauce

Shredded cheese

Note

When I buy tomato paste, I prefer a product with no added salt. If yours does have salt, be sure to adjust the seasoning in the recipe accordingly. And while this recipe calls for ground turkey, you could also use ground beef.

3 tablespoons extra-virgin olive oil

1 pound ground turkey

1 tablespoon tomato paste

2 teaspoons kosher salt

1 teaspoon paprika

¼ teaspoon freshly ground black pepper

1 medium yellow onion, diced (about 1 cup)

4 garlic cloves, minced

1¼ cups prepared or store-bought tomato sauce

2 tablespoons light brown sugar

1 teaspoon yellow mustard

1 cup shredded cheese (I like yellow cheddar here)

1 heaping cup cornbread roughly broken up into small pieces

- Set a baking rack 6 to 7 inches from the broiler. Preheat the oven to the low broil setting.

- Heat the oil in a 10- or 12-inch cast-iron pan (or other ovenproof pan) over medium heat. Add the turkey, tomato paste, salt, paprika, and pepper and use a wooden spoon to break up the turkey into smaller pieces. Cook, stirring constantly, until the liquid released by the turkey has evaporated and the meat has browned, about 10 minutes. Add the onion and garlic and cook until the onion has softened and begins to brown, about another 3 minutes. Stir in the tomato sauce, brown sugar, and mustard and bring the mixture to a simmer. Cook until the mixture has thickened (the wooden spoon should leave a trail behind it when you stir), 5 to 6 minutes. Remove the pan from the heat and sprinkle ½ cup of the shredded cheddar over the top. Set aside.

- In a small bowl, combine the cornbread and the remaining ½ cup shredded cheddar, using your hands to gently combine them. Top the skillet with the cornbread mixture and place it under the broiler for 4 to 5 minutes, until the cheese is melted, the cornbread is deep golden brown in spots, and the Sloppy Joe mixture is bubbling around the edges. Let it rest for 5 minutes before scooping into a bowl and serving.

Pasta, Beans, Rice, & Potatoes

These ingredients are some of the most hardworking in the kitchen. They're craving satisfiers, inexpensive fillers, and inoffensive offerings to the pickiest of eaters. I think all my kids ate for an entire year of their lives was potatoes and pasta, and they've now, thankfully, moved on to accepting beans and rice on their plates too. But no matter how carefully I plan, I always end up with at least one container of leftovers in the fridge. And I don't care how well you know how to cook rice/pasta/potatoes/beans, those things are just not as enjoyable the next day, even when they're reheated. They get dry, crumbly, bland, and, well, starchy. BUT, there's a solution for that! With just the right kind of treatment, you can turn that well-intentioned surplus into new family favorites.

Buffalo Chicken Bean Dip

I don't usually need much of an excuse to make this dip because it's over-the-top delicious, but whenever I find myself with a random assortment of canned beans in the pantry—which somehow I always do!—then it's definitely the right occasion. This recipe calls for the usual suspects of a good buffalo chicken dip—ranch dressing, cheese, buffalo sauce—but the surprise element is the thick, creamy consistency that the beans give to the dish. This is also another great recipe for using up leftover cooked chicken!

1 (15-ounce) can cannellini beans, drained and rinsed

½ cup Tangy Ranch Dressing (page 168) or store-bought ranch dressing

1 teaspoon kosher salt

¼ cup cilantro leaves, finely chopped

2 cups shredded Monterey Jack cheese

1 (15-ounce) can pinto beans, drained

¼ cup hot sauce of choice (I love Calabama Hot Sauce!)

3 tablespoons unsalted butter, melted

1 cup shredded cooked chicken

¼ cup pickled jalapeños, roughly chopped (my favorite is Jed's)

Sour cream and onion chips, tortilla chips, corn chips, and/or sliced baguette, for serving

Note

The recipe calls for cannellini and pinto beans, but I've found that most mild-tasting beans work well here. Feel free to experiment and mix and match!

- Set an oven rack 6 to 7 inches from the broiler. Preheat the oven to 400°F.
- In the bowl of a food processor, combine the cannellini beans, ranch dressing, and salt. Puree until smooth. Add the cilantro and pulse a few times to just incorporate but not break down the cilantro any further. Pour the pureed bean mixture into a large bowl and fold in 1½ cups of the cheese and the pinto beans. Set aside.
- In a medium bowl, whisk together the hot sauce and melted butter. Add the shredded chicken and toss to coat. Fold the chicken mixture into the bean mixture and spread everything evenly in a 1½-quart casserole dish. Bake for 15 minutes, or until the cheese has melted and the dip has warmed through.
- Switch the oven to the low broil setting.
- Top the bean dip with the pickled jalapeños and the remaining ½ cup cheese. Broil for 5 minutes, or until the cheese is melted and charring in spots and the bean dip is bubbling around the edges. Let cool for 10 minutes before serving with chips.

Chicken Bone Soup

with Rice

One of my mom's signature moves was to make us roast chicken one night and then boil the bones down for broth the next. I remember her even scooping up any bones from our plates to toss in too—after all, they were getting boiled! Is making chicken soup out of chicken bones a new idea? Nope. Are there still *way* too many chicken carcasses being needlessly sent to the trash or stashed indefinitely in the freezer anyway? Yep! So, finally, here is your go-to recipe for the most luxurious chicken soup that you can make with nothing more than dinner scraps, including cooked rice (or pasta) and roasted vegetables.

Fresh cilantro

Fresh ginger

Frozen veggies

Bone Broth

1 chicken carcass (about 1¼ pounds)

1 small yellow onion, quartered

¼ cup packed fresh cilantro stems and leaves

2 (3-inch) pieces fresh ginger, thinly sliced (about ¼ cup)

1 (4-inch) piece fresh turmeric, thinly sliced (about ¼ cup; optional)

3 garlic cloves, smashed

1 cinnamon stick

2 star anise pods

1 teaspoon whole black peppercorns

6 whole cloves

To Assemble

1 tablespoon soy sauce

2 teaspoons kosher salt, plus more to taste

1 teaspoon toasted sesame oil

1½ cups chopped frozen or roasted vegetables, such as zucchini, carrots, fennel, peas, yellow squash, onions, or parsnips

1 cup cooked rice or pasta

1 cup shredded cooked chicken (optional)

2 teaspoons fresh lime juice

Fresh cilantro leaves, for serving

Note

If you don't have leftover rice or noodles, you can cook some separately and add to the soup as it finishes.

- **Make the bone broth:** In a 3-quart pot or Dutch oven over medium-high heat, combine the chicken bones, onion, cilantro, ginger, turmeric (if using), garlic, cinnamon stick, star anise, peppercorns, and cloves with 10 cups water. Bring to a boil and reduce to a simmer over medium-low heat. Cook the broth for 1 hour.

- Remove the pot from the heat and strain the broth through a fine-mesh sieve or colander. Discard the bones and aromatics. Add the broth back to the pot if making the soup right away. If using later, let the broth cool completely and store in an airtight container in the refrigerator for about a week, or freeze for up to 6 months.

- **Assemble the soup:** In a 3-quart pot or Dutch oven over medium heat, bring the broth to a simmer. Stir in the soy sauce, salt, and sesame oil. Add the vegetables, rice, and chicken, if using. Continue to simmer until all the ingredients are reheated, about 6 minutes. Stir in the lime juice and season with salt to taste. Divide the soup among four serving bowls and garnish with the cilantro.

Yesterday's Crispy Rice Cakes

My whole family loves Chinese, Japanese, Indian, and Mexican takeout, which means we usually have at least one or two containers of leftover rice in the fridge. Most of the time I end up feeding it to our chickens because no one seems too interested in plain, slightly dried-out white rice. Shocking, I know! But I always wish it had a little more dinner mileage. It turns out that leftover slightly dried-out rice—any type—is perfect for forming into cakes and frying until crispy. The cakes themselves are meal-worthy, or you can top them with your favorite sushi-inspired toppings such as sushi-grade raw fish, wasabi paste, pickled ginger, seaweed salad, julienned veggies, or spicy mayo.

Egg whites

1 large egg white

2 cups cooked white or brown rice

3 tablespoons cornstarch

1 tablespoon soy sauce

1 tablespoon furikake (optional; see Notes)

Vegetable oil, for frying

Kosher salt

Your favorite sushi toppings, such as sushi-grade fish, wasabi paste, pickled ginger, seaweed salad, thinly sliced vegetables, sliced avocado, and/or spicy mayo, for serving

- Line a baking sheet with parchment paper. Line a second baking sheet with paper towels. Set aside.
- In a medium bowl, whisk the egg white until frothy. Add the rice, cornstarch, soy sauce, and furikake, if using. Stir to coat the rice, breaking up any lumps if necessary. Using a ¼-ounce ice cream scoop, scoop and pack the rice and drop it onto the parchment-lined baking sheet. Repeat until you have 10 rice cakes. Alternatively, you can use a tablespoon rather than an ice cream scoop to create 10 (2-tablespoon) cakes.
- Lightly wet your hands and pack each cake into a ½-inch-thick square, round, or any other shape you like. (Cookie cutters work great here!) Place the cakes back on the baking sheet and cover with plastic wrap. Refrigerate for 30 minutes.
- Heat a large sauté pan over medium-high heat. Add enough vegetable oil to come about ¼ inch up the sides of the pan and heat until the oil shimmers or registers 350°F on a thermometer. Working in batches so as not to overcrowd the pan, add the rice cakes and cook until golden and crispy, about 1 minute per side. Use a slotted spoon or spatula to transfer the cakes to the paper towel–lined baking sheet. Immediately sprinkle them with salt. Top with your favorite sushi ingredients and enjoy.

Notes

You can use cookie cutters to add creative shapes to these rice cakes. Regardless of how you shape them, make sure to keep your hands damp when handling the rice, which will keep the rice from sticking.

This recipe calls for furikake, which is one of my favorite seasonings. It's a Japanese blend that typically includes toasted sesame seeds, nori, salt, and sugar. You can sprinkle it on just about anything savory (fish, eggs, rice, veggies), and it lasts forever in your pantry.

Mashed Potato Dumpling Soup

Mashed potatoes are a weeknight staple at my house (especially my Buttermilk Horseradish Mashed Potatoes, page 173), so there's always some left over in my refrigerator. While no one would complain about having them reheated with a dollop of butter, I discovered that I could use that mash as the base for lighter-than-air dumplings in a flavorful vegetable-studded broth. This is a particularly great recipe to reach for after Thanksgiving when you have more mashed potatoes than you know what to do with and you wouldn't mind a reset in the veggie department.

Fresh parsley

Fresh dill

Green cabbage

Carrots

3 tablespoons unsalted butter

1 medium yellow onion, diced (about 1 cup)

1 large egg yolk

1½ teaspoons kosher salt, plus more to taste

Freshly ground black pepper

¾ cup prepared mashed potatoes, chilled

¼ cup all-purpose flour, plus more as needed

2 tablespoons extra-virgin olive oil, plus more for serving

½ small head green cabbage, cored and cut into 1-inch pieces (about 6 cups)

4 cups low-sodium chicken or vegetable stock

1 large carrot, peeled and cut into ¼-inch rounds (about 1 cup)

1 cup fresh parsley leaves

2 tablespoons fresh dill, torn, for serving

● Melt the butter in a large saucepan or Dutch oven over medium-low heat. Add the onion and cook, stirring often to prevent the onion from browning too quickly, until softened and caramelized, about 10 minutes. Remove the pot from the heat and set aside.

● In a medium bowl, whisk together the egg yolk, ½ teaspoon of the salt, and a few grinds of pepper until combined. Fold in the mashed potatoes, using a rubber spatula or wooden spoon to press the mixture into the bottom of the bowl and break up any lumps in the potato to reach a smooth texture. Fold in 2 tablespoons of the flour and again mix, pressing the mixture into the bottom of the bowl to ensure there are no lumps. Continue adding the flour, 1 tablespoon at a time, until the potatoes have a firm texture. They should hold a stiff peak when lifting them out of the bowl. If your potatoes are very loose, add more flour 1 tablespoon at a time. Fold in the caramelized onions. Refrigerate the mixture for at least 30 minutes, or up to overnight.

● In the same saucepan you used for the onions, heat the oil over medium heat. Add the cabbage and ½ teaspoon of the salt and toss to coat with the oil. Cook until the cabbage has wilted and browned around the edges, about 6 minutes. Stir in the stock and 4 cups water, scraping the bottom of the pan with a wooden spoon to release any brown bits. Add the carrot and parsley and bring the mixture to a boil over high heat. Add ½ teaspoon of the salt and a few grinds of black pepper. Reduce the heat to medium-low and simmer the broth until the carrots are just cooked through and tender, 10 to 12 minutes. Reduce the heat to low so the soup is barely simmering at the edges of the pan. Taste the broth and season with more salt, if needed.

● Wet a soup spoon with water and scoop up 1 heaping tablespoon of the potato mixture. Gently drop the mixture into the soup. Repeat forming the dumplings (you should have about 16) and adding them to the pot, taking care not to add them too close to one another or they'll stick together. If the dumplings start to fall apart, reduce the heat even more. Cook the dumplings until they are heated all the way through and float to the top of the soup, 5 to 6 minutes. Gently ladle the soup into four serving bowls and garnish with dill and a drizzle of olive oil.

Mashed Potato Dumpling Soup
PAGE 42

Ciao, Arancini

To me, a dish gets major points if it comes together easily, is flexible for flavoring up with whatever I happen to be in the mood for or have on hand, *and* the kids will happily eat it. That's why risotto is one of my all-time favorite meals on my dinner roster (and scored a spot in my first book). I wanted to take this love a step further by including a recipe that you can reach for to use up any leftovers *or* if you decide to double your original batch of risotto and enjoy it later in the week (a major time-saver). Arancini—or fried rice balls—are actually traditionally made from leftover risotto. They come together in minutes and, as an added bonus, you can add any cheese, breadcrumbs, or tomato sauce that's looking for a good use.

Fresh basil or parsley

Breadcrumbs

Melting cheese, such as Gruyère, fontina, mozzarella, Swiss, or provolone

Tomato sauce

Nonstick cooking spray

3 large eggs

2 cups prepared risotto, chilled

Kosher salt

2 tablespoons roughly chopped fresh basil or parsley leaves

¼ cup all-purpose flour

1 cup plain, seasoned, or panko breadcrumbs

12 (¼-inch) cubes melting cheese, such as Gruyère, fontina, mozzarella, Swiss, or provolone (about 4 ounces)

Warmed prepared or store-bought tomato sauce, with or without meat, for dipping

- Preheat the oven to 400°F. Line a baking sheet with parchment paper and spray with nonstick spray. Set aside.
- In a large bowl, whisk 1 of the eggs. Taste the risotto and add salt as needed, then fold it into the egg. Fold in the herbs so everything is evenly combined. Set aside.
- Add the flour to a shallow dish. In a second dish, beat the remaining 2 eggs. In a third dish, add the breadcrumbs. Scoop 2 heaping tablespoons of the risotto mixture into your palm. Gently press the risotto into a disk and place a cube of cheese in the center. Fold the risotto over the cheese and form a tight ball. Dredge the risotto ball by first lightly coating it in flour, followed by the egg. Let the excess drip off before coating it in the breadcrumbs. Place the assembled arancini on the prepared baking sheet and repeat with the remaining risotto. Spray the tops of the arancini with nonstick spray.
- Bake for 15 minutes, or until the arancini are beginning to brown. Flip and bake until the arancini are golden brown and crispy all over, an additional 12 to 15 minutes. Serve with warmed tomato sauce for dipping.

Clear-Out-the-Fridge Pasta Salad

with Charred Tomato Dressing

Consider this my ode to the macaroni salad of my youth. Yes, my mother's gold-standard version was heavy on the mayo and light on the veggies, but the sentiment was the same—an easy, crowd-pleasing dish that puts cold pasta *and* leftover cooked vegetables to work. The secret is the smoky, anchovy-flecked charred tomato dressing, which infuses all the ingredients with complex, savory flavor.

Anchovies

Fresh herbs

Roasted or grilled veggies

2 vine-ripened tomatoes

6 garlic cloves, unpeeled

2 teaspoons vegetable oil

2 anchovy fillets (optional, though they give the salad a nice, salty zip)

1 teaspoon dried oregano leaves or 1 tablespoon fresh oregano leaves

1 teaspoon kosher salt, plus more to taste

½ teaspoon Calabrian chili paste or red chili flakes

1 cup packed fresh herbs, such as basil and parsley, roughly chopped

1 tablespoon aged balsamic vinegar

1 tablespoon fresh lemon juice (about ½ lemon)

1 tablespoon extra-virgin olive oil

4 heaping cups cooked pasta (see Note)

3 cups roasted or grilled vegetables, cut into ½-inch pieces

1 cup mozzarella pearls, cubed mozzarella, torn burrata, or shaved Parmesan cheese

Freshly ground black pepper

- Place an oven rack 6 to 7 inches from the broiler. Preheat the oven to a low broil.

- Place the tomatoes and garlic on a baking sheet and toss with the vegetable oil until well coated. Broil for 10 minutes, or until the tomatoes are just beginning to burst and the garlic is tender. Let cool completely.

- Squeeze the garlic cloves out of their skins and add the cloves to a mortar and pestle along with the anchovies, oregano, salt, and chili paste. Grind the mixture into a coarse paste. Add the tomatoes and their juices and mash until the tomatoes are broken into smaller pieces and a sauce has formed. Stir in the herbs, vinegar, lemon juice, and olive oil. Set aside. (If you don't have a mortar and pestle, you can mince the garlic and anchovies on a cutting board, then add the oregano, salt, and chili paste and use the side of a knife to create a paste. Add the paste and tomatoes to a bowl and mash the tomatoes with the back of a spoon.)

- In a large bowl, combine the pasta, vegetables, and cheese and toss to combine. Pour the charred tomato dressing over the top, fold together until everything is evenly coated, and season with salt and black pepper to taste. Serve immediately or refrigerate overnight. The longer the pasta salad sits in the sauce, the more flavor it will absorb.

Note

The great thing about this recipe is that it works with *any* kind of pasta, from orzo to penne to rigatoni to spaghetti. If you're anticipating having leftover pasta, be sure to cool it completely or even run it under cold water before storing it in an airtight container. This will ensure that it doesn't become one big clump of pasta. If you want to make this salad without having leftovers, prepare 1 (16-ounce) box of pasta. If you don't have any leftover grilled vegetables, you can make a quick and easy batch by chopping up any raw vegetables you have in the fridge, cutting them into ½-inch pieces, and tossing them in olive oil with a pinch of salt and pepper. Place each kind of vegetable on its own section of a baking sheet and roast at 425°F until the vegetables are tender and deeply browned. By separating each vegetable, you can remove them from the pan as they finish, since they'll likely need different amounts of time.

Spaghetti Pie, Oh My!

To be perfectly honest, most of the time when I'm making pasta and red sauce for dinner, it's with the anticipation of having this dish later in the week. Something magical happens when the starchy leftover pasta binds with the sauce, which lends itself perfectly to frying up into a sliceable pie with a golden, caramelized crust. I love serving this with a simple side salad of arugula dressed with lemon vinaigrette and plenty of grated Parm.

Fresh basil

3 large eggs

½ cup grated Parmesan cheese

¼ cup tightly packed fresh basil leaves, roughly chopped

2 tablespoons heavy cream

¼ teaspoon freshly ground black pepper

Pinch of kosher salt (optional)

3 heaping cups cold spaghetti in tomato sauce

¼ cup plus 1 tablespoon extra-virgin olive oil

- In a medium bowl, whisk together the eggs, cheese, basil, cream, and pepper until well combined. Taste your leftover spaghetti before adding it to the egg mixture. If it could use some salt, add a good pinch to the egg mixture. Use tongs or your hands to toss the spaghetti in the egg mixture, making sure every strand is coated.

- In a 6- or 8-inch nonstick sauté pan over medium-low heat, heat ¼ cup of the oil and gently swirl the pan to coat the bottom and edges. Heat until you see ripples in the oil, about 1 minute. Carefully add the spaghetti, making sure to place it in an even layer all the way to the edge of the pan. Cook until the bottom is golden brown and crispy when you lift up an edge with a spatula, 7 to 8 minutes. Remove the pan from the heat.

- Jiggle the pan slightly to make sure the bottom of the pie is completely released. Flip the spaghetti pie onto a baking sheet, making sure to tilt the pan away from you to avoid any oil splatter. Place the pan back over medium-low heat and add the remaining 1 tablespoon oil. Slide the pie back into the pan and cook until brown and crispy on the second side, about 6 more minutes. Turn out the spaghetti pie onto a plate or cutting board. Cut into quarters and serve.

Mimi's Chicken & Rice Casserole

It doesn't get more retro than a casserole, especially one featuring a can of condensed cream of mushroom soup (I couldn't resist!). There's a reason these layered, baked, one-dish meals have never really gone out of style: They're nourishing, soul-warming, and usually enjoyed by everyone at the table. The beauty of this recipe in particular is that the leftover rice reconstitutes in the soup, giving it a creamy, risotto-like texture.

Cremini mushrooms

Dry white wine (such as pinot grigio or sauvignon blanc)

Low-sodium chicken stock

Fresh parsley

Note

This recipe is flexible with how much rice you can use, so you can adapt it to suit your leftovers. And be sure to save your broccoli stems for Creamy Broccoli Soup (page 122)!

4 bone-in, skin-on chicken thighs (about 2 pounds)

Kosher salt and freshly ground black pepper

2 tablespoons extra-virgin olive oil, plus more for drizzling

1 small head broccoli, cut into small florets (about 1 heaping cup; see Note)

8 cremini mushrooms, stemmed and quartered

¼ cup dry white wine, such as pinot grigio or sauvignon blanc

1 (10.5-ounce) can condensed cream of mushroom soup

½ cup low-sodium chicken stock

2 cups cooked wild, brown, or white rice (see Note)

¼ cup grated Parmesan cheese

¼ cup fresh parsley leaves, roughly chopped

- Preheat the oven to 375°F.

- Generously season the skin side of the thighs with salt and pepper. Heat the oil in a large sauté or cast-iron pan over medium heat. Add the chicken to the pan skin side down. Season the other side of the thighs with salt and pepper. Sear the chicken until the skin releases from the pan and is a deep golden brown, about 5 minutes. Flip and sear on the second side until golden brown, about an additional 5 minutes. Transfer the chicken to an 8 x 8-inch baking dish.

- Discard all but 1 tablespoon of the rendered chicken fat and oil from the skillet. Add the broccoli and mushrooms and toss to coat. Transfer the vegetables to the baking dish with the chicken. (Do not rinse or wipe out the pan.) Bake for 15 minutes, or until the chicken is cooked through and the vegetables have browned. Transfer the chicken thighs to a plate. Keep the vegetables in the baking dish and the oven on.

- Place the original sauté pan back over medium heat. Add the wine and use a wooden spoon to scrape up any brown bits from the bottom of the pan. Allow the wine to reduce for about 1 minute. Transfer the wine and any browned bits to a medium bowl. Whisk in the condensed soup and chicken stock. Fold in the rice and Parmesan, making sure to break up any bits of rice that are sticking together. Add the roasted vegetables and any liquid in the baking dish. Return the mixture to the baking dish and top with the chicken thighs, skin side up. Sprinkle with the parsley and drizzle with olive oil.

- Bake for 25 minutes, or until the mixture is bubbling around the edges and the vegetables are cooked through. Let rest for 15 minutes before serving.

Mean Bean Burgers

with Saffron Yogurt Sauce

Whether you have an extra can of black beans in your pantry or leftover cooked beans (like my Cuban-Style Black Beans from *Pull Up a Chair*), this recipe will convert even the most skeptical bean eater. It yields the perfect hearty patty, which becomes a serious contender for "Best (Vegan) Burger" when drizzled with a tangy saffron-infused nondairy yogurt sauce and loaded up on a bun with avocado. These would also be great served over rice or greens.

Low-sodium vegetable stock

Rolled oats

Raw, unsalted almonds

Fresh parsley and cilantro

Plain whole-milk yogurt, Greek yogurt, or nondairy yogurt

Black Bean Burgers

½ cup low-sodium vegetable stock

½ cup rolled oats

2 tablespoons extra-virgin olive oil

⅓ cup raw, unsalted almonds

2 tablespoons roughly chopped fresh parsley

1 teaspoon smoked paprika

1 teaspoon ground cumin

1 teaspoon ground coriander

1 teaspoon garlic powder

¼ teaspoon kosher salt

¼ teaspoon freshly ground black pepper

1¼ cups cooked black beans, drained completely of excess liquid; or 1 (15-ounce) can black beans, drained and rinsed

Yogurt Sauce

½ cup plain whole-milk yogurt, Greek yogurt, or nondairy yogurt

2 dates, pitted and finely chopped

1 tablespoon roughly chopped fresh cilantro

½ teaspoon kosher salt

¼ teaspoon saffron threads

¼ teaspoon ground turmeric

To Assemble

Kosher salt and freshly ground black pepper

Extra-virgin olive oil

4 brioche hamburger buns (or any other type of bun), toasted if desired

1 avocado, peeled, pitted, and thinly sliced

4 fried eggs (optional)

● **Make the burgers:** In a microwave-safe bowl or a small saucepan, heat the vegetable stock until just steaming, about 1 minute in a microwave or about 2 minutes over medium-high heat. Add the oats to a medium bowl. Pour the stock over the oats and soak until the oats have absorbed most of the stock and are soft, 10 to 12 minutes. Strain out any excess liquid and set aside.

● In a small sauté pan over medium-low heat, combine the olive oil and almonds. Cook, stirring occasionally, until the nuts are deeply toasted, about 4 minutes. Stir in the parsley and remove the pan from the heat. Stir in the paprika, cumin, coriander, and garlic powder. The spices will toast slightly from the residual heat.

CONTINUES

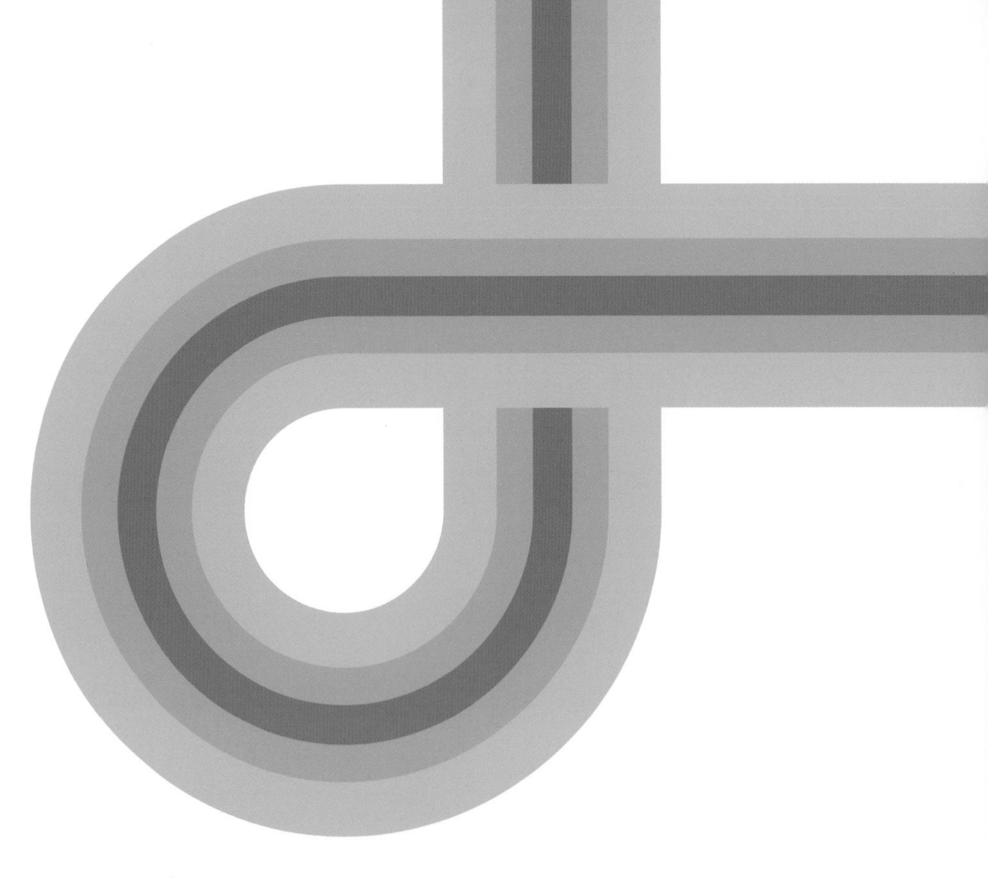

Note

Another option is to turn the burger mixture into meatballs. Just make smaller rounds and fry them in a nonstick pan.

- In the bowl of a food processor, add the nut and spice mixture, salt, and pepper, and pulse until coarsely ground. Add the oats and process until the mixture forms a ball. Add the black beans and pulse until the mixture just comes together. It's okay if some of the beans haven't completely broken down; this will add some texture to your burgers.

- Line a baking sheet with parchment paper. Using damp hands to prevent sticking, form the black bean mixture into 4 equal balls and place them on the prepared baking sheet. Press down on each ball to flatten it into a ¼-inch-thick patty. Cover the baking sheet with plastic wrap and refrigerate for at least 30 minutes, or up to overnight.

- **Make the yogurt sauce:** In a medium bowl, whisk together the yogurt, dates, cilantro, salt, saffron, and turmeric. Use immediately, or store in an airtight container in the refrigerator for up to 3 days.

- **Assemble:** Season the top of each patty with salt and pepper.

- In a large nonstick sauté pan over medium-low heat, add enough oil to lightly coat the pan. Place the burgers salt-and-peppered side down and season the second side with salt and pepper. (You may need to cook them in batches to avoid crowding the pan.) Cook until the burgers form a deeply caramelized crust, 3 to 4 minutes. Flip and repeat on the other side. Remove the pan from the heat.

- Lay out all the bottom burger buns on a clean work surface. Spread about 1 tablespoon of the yogurt sauce on each bun. Top with a burger patty, followed by ¼ of the sliced avocado, another tablespoon of the sauce, and a fried egg, if desired. Add the top bun and serve immediately.

Fish & Tot Sandwiches

I often have a half-empty bag of tater tots left in the freezer after making a quick brunch or dinner side dish, and so I made it my mission to figure out a way to use them besides serving them alongside chicken nuggets (shame-free zone here!). Then I discovered it: the tot-waffle, the perfect combo of hash and waffle. I suppose I could have stopped there, but then I decided to riff on fish-and-chips by topping a waffle with crispy fried fish smothered in a tangy slaw and a maple-chili sauce. Although, you could skip the fish and just use the waffles in place of bread for cold-cut sandwiches.

Red onion

Shredded cheese

Scallions

Cabbage (red or green)

Fresh cilantro

Waffles

2½ cups cooked or defrosted tater tots

¼ medium red onion, grated and squeezed of excess liquid (about 2 tablespoons)

¼ teaspoon kosher salt

¼ teaspoon freshly ground black pepper

2 large eggs, beaten

1 cup shredded cheese (I like cheddar for this)

Nonstick spray

Slaw

¼ cup mayonnaise

1½ teaspoons maple syrup

2 teaspoons of your favorite hot sauce, or to taste

1½ cups thinly sliced cabbage (green, red, or a mixture of both)

1 scallion (white and green parts), thinly sliced (2 to 3 tablespoons)

Maple Syrup Chili Sauce

¼ cup maple syrup

2 tablespoons light brown sugar

¼ teaspoon kosher salt

1 small Fresno pepper or red jalapeño, seeded and finely minced (about 3 tablespoons)

1 tablespoon chopped cilantro leaves

1 teaspoon fresh lime juice

Fried Fish

½ cup store-bought tempura batter mix

2 (4- to 6-ounce) skinless whitefish fillets, such as cod, haddock, flounder, or tilapia

Vegetable oil, for frying

Kosher salt

- **Make the waffles:** In a large bowl, use your hands to mash the tater tots until they're the consistency of hash browns. Mix in the onion, salt, and pepper. Add the eggs and mix until all the potatoes are evenly coated. Fold in the cheese and set aside.

- Preheat your waffle iron to the medium setting and spray with nonstick spray. Add 1 packed cup of the waffle mixture and cook until the waffles are deeply golden brown and easily release from the pan, about 12 minutes. (You may need to add more or less of the mixture, depending on the size of your waffle iron. The goal is to make waffles that are about 1 inch thick.) Try not to check the waffles for at least 8 minutes, or you will possibly tear them. To keep the finished waffles warm while you make the rest of the components, wrap them in foil or place them on a baking sheet in a 200°F oven.

CONTINUES

Note

This recipe makes two large open-faced sandwiches, which is what you'll get from about ¼ to ½ bag of tots. Should you want more sandwiches, you can easily double the recipe. You can also make the slaw and maple-chili sauce ahead if you want to prep before serving.

- **Make the slaw:** In a small bowl, whisk together the mayonnaise, maple syrup, and hot sauce. If you don't like things too spicy, add 1 teaspoon of the hot sauce at a time until you reach your desired heat level, or omit entirely. Set aside.

- In a medium bowl, toss together the cabbage and scallion. Add the dressing and toss again. This can be made up to 4 hours in advance and stored in the refrigerator.

- **Make the maple-chili sauce:** In a small saucepan over medium heat, combine the maple syrup, brown sugar, and salt. Bring to a simmer and stir until the sugar and salt have dissolved, about 1 minute. Remove the pot from the heat and stir in the pepper, cilantro, and lime juice. Use immediately or let cool to store in an airtight container in the refrigerator for up to 4 days.

- **Make the fried fish:** Line a baking sheet with paper towels and set aside.

- Prepare the tempura batter mix according to package directions. Batter the fish and set aside.

- Heat a large sauté or cast-iron pan over medium-high heat. Add enough oil to come halfway up the sides and heat until the oil shimmers or registers 375°F on a thermometer. Add the fish and cook until golden brown, crispy, and cooked through, 6 to 8 minutes, depending on the thickness of your fish. Use tongs or a slotted spoon to transfer the fish to the prepared baking sheet and immediately sprinkle with salt.

- To assemble each sandwich, place one waffle on a plate and top it with a scoop of the slaw, a piece of fried fish, and a drizzling of maple-chili sauce. Eat immediately.

Lemon Polenta Flapjacks

This recipe is not so much a use for leftover polenta as it is a solution for that pesky bag of cornmeal, grits, or polenta that always seems to be hanging out in my pantry. It's usually the aftermath of a hankering for cornbread (see Cornbread Skillet Sloppy Joes, page 32) or a weeknight polenta dinner, but after the first couple of uses, there's not enough in the bag for an entire meal—and yet I don't want to throw it away. Enter this recipe for these sweet, bright pancakes that get a punch from lemon and a creamy texture from ricotta and cornmeal. It's a fun twist on your usual morning offerings or even dessert, and you get to make room in your pantry for something new!

Whole-milk ricotta

3 large eggs

1 cup whole-milk ricotta

2 tablespoons cane sugar

Zest of 1 lemon

2 teaspoons fresh lemon juice

1 teaspoon almond extract

¼ cup plus 2 tablespoons all-purpose flour

¼ cup polenta (yellow corn grits)

1 teaspoon baking powder

1 teaspoon baking soda

4 tablespoons unsalted butter, plus more for serving

Rescue-Those-Berries Preserves (page 128) and/or maple syrup

- In a medium bowl, whisk together the eggs, ricotta, sugar, lemon zest and juice, and almond extract until smooth. Fold in the flour, polenta, baking powder, and baking soda until just combined and you no longer see any dry bits. Let the batter sit for 20 minutes to allow the polenta to soften.

- Heat a large cast-iron pan, griddle pan, or nonstick sauté pan over medium-low heat until the pan just begins to smoke, 2 to 3 minutes. Add 1 tablespoon of the butter and swirl the pan as it melts to evenly coat the bottom. Working in batches so as not to overcrowd the pan, add ⅓ cup of the batter per pancake. Gently shimmy the pan to help the pancakes settle into even shapes or use an offset spatula to gently press them down. Cook until the pancakes are deeply browned on the bottom and bubbles appear around the edges, about 2 minutes. Flip the pancakes and cook until the second side is a deep brown, about another 2 minutes. Transfer to a plate and repeat with the remaining batter, making sure to add more butter between batches. If the pan gets too hot, remove it from the heat and let it cool before continuing.

- Serve with butter, preserves, and/or maple syrup.

Lemon Polenta Flapjacks
PAGE 61

A FAMILY TRADITION SINCE
1887
LOG CABIN
NO HIGH FRUCTOSE CORN SYRUP
NO ARTIFICIAL FLAVORS
Original
SYRUP
LOVED LOVED LOVED

Chocolate Spud Cake

Yes, you read that right. A rich, fudgy chocolate cake made with the secret ingredient of none other than a leftover plain baked potato. The starchy vegetable works wonders for giving fudgy body to this cake, which, if you ask me, is a much more respectable destiny than getting soggy in the fridge. It makes me wonder why I don't make more baked potatoes...For a cheeky twist, decorate this cake with potato chips!

Buttermilk

Bittersweet or semisweet chocolate

Potato chips

Cake

½ cup vegetable oil, plus more for greasing

1½ cups all-purpose flour, plus more for dusting

2 cups cane sugar

1 cup unsweetened cocoa powder

1½ teaspoons baking soda

1½ teaspoons baking powder

3 large eggs

1¾ cups buttermilk

1 large baked potato, skin removed and roughly chopped (about 1½ cups)

1 tablespoon pure vanilla paste or extract

1 teaspoon instant espresso powder

Frosting

4 ounces bittersweet or semisweet chocolate, finely chopped (about ½ cup)

2 sticks (1 cup) unsalted butter, at room temperature

1½ cups confectioners' sugar

½ cup unsweetened cocoa powder

¼ cup buttermilk

2 teaspoons pure vanilla paste or extract

Potato chips and/or chocolate curls, for serving (optional)

- **Make the cake:** Preheat the oven to 350°F.

- Lightly grease two 8-inch cake pans with vegetable oil. Line each with a parchment round and grease with a little more oil over the parchment. Lightly dust the inside of both pans with flour and tap out any excess. Set aside.

- In a large bowl, whisk together the sugar, flour, cocoa powder, baking soda, and baking powder. Set aside.

- In a blender, combine the eggs, buttermilk, oil, potato, vanilla, and espresso powder. Blend on medium speed until completely combined and smooth. Using a rubber spatula, gently fold the mixture into the sugar and flour mixture until smooth and you no longer see any dry bits. Divide the batter between the two prepared pans.

- Bake for 55 minutes to 1 hour, until a paring knife or skewer inserted into the center comes out clean. Let the cakes cool in the pans for 20 minutes, or until cool enough to handle. Run a paring knife around the edges to release the cakes and transfer them to a cooling rack or parchment-lined baking sheet. Allow the cakes to cool completely while you make the frosting.

CONTINUES

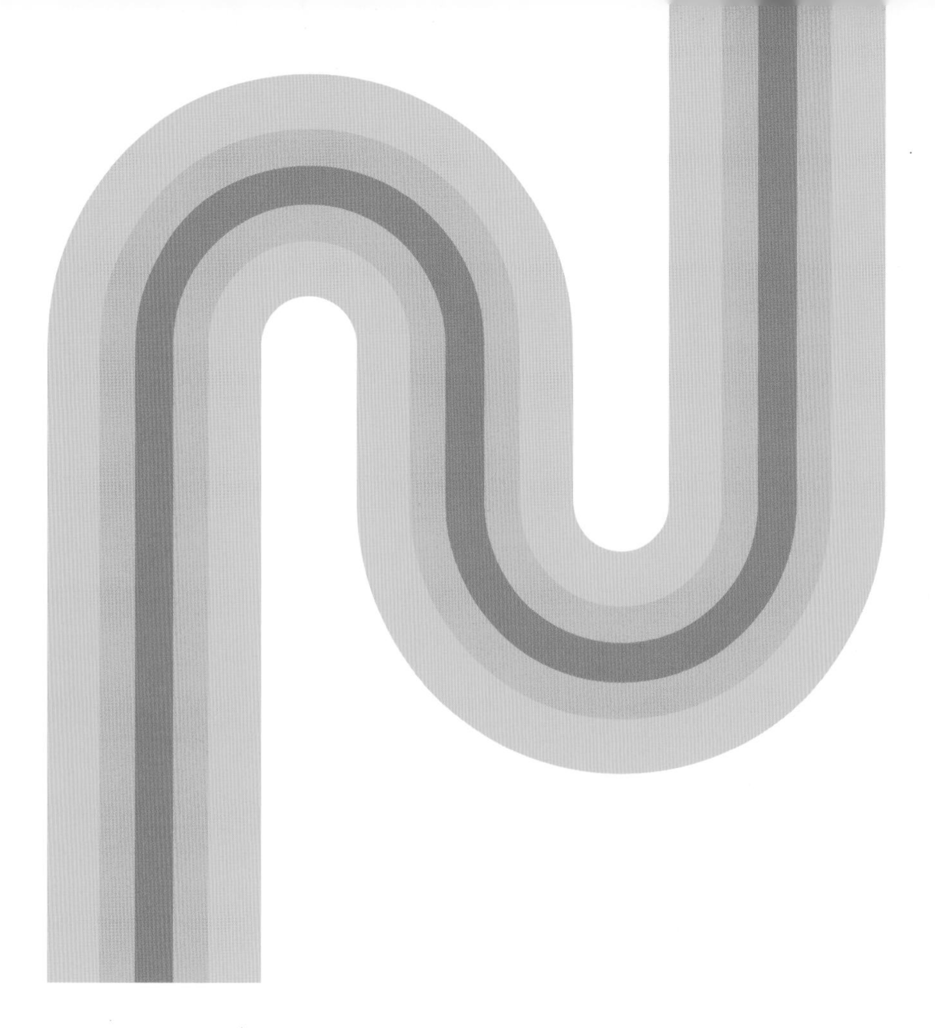

- **Make the frosting:** In a microwave-safe bowl, microwave the chocolate for 30 seconds. Stir, then microwave in 20-second increments until the chocolate is just melted and smooth. Set aside to cool.

- In the bowl of a stand mixer fitted with the paddle attachment or a large bowl with a hand mixer, add the butter. Beat on high speed until the butter is lighter in color and fluffy. Sift in the confectioners' sugar and cocoa powder. Using a rubber spatula, fold the sugar and cocoa powder into the butter until just combined. Add the buttermilk and vanilla and beat on low speed until incorporated. Increase the speed to high and mix until well combined and smooth. Pour in the melted chocolate and mix on low speed until just combined.

- **Assemble:** If necessary, use a large serrated knife to trim the tops of the cakes to make them flat. (This will help you build a more even cake.) Top one cake with enough frosting to create a ¼-inch layer (about 1½ cups). Using an offset spatula or butter knife, smooth the frosting so it is even and reaches the edges of the cake. Top with the second cake, with the flatter of the two sides facing up (usually the bottom of the cake). Add the remaining frosting and use the offset spatula or knife to frost the entire cake. Decorate with the potato chips and/or chocolate curls, if using. Serve immediately or store at room temperature for a few hours until ready to serve.

Meat & Fish

Growing up, being in the kitchen with my mom was a lesson in economy. She perfected the art of keeping a rotation of simple, inexpensive ingredients in the house. As for meat and fish—which could get a little pricey—she would watch for a good deal, then store her findings in the freezer. And whenever she would prepare a meal, it was never for just the five of us. Watching her cook, you'd think there were twice as many coming to dinner. But that's only because she was also as smart with her time as she was with her budget. She knew that if she was going to make the effort to make a meal, she might as well make enough to double as that week's lunch or the next night's dinner. That woman was a life hack expert before life hacks were a thing! But she also knew that as much as we kids loved our Tuna Helper, beef stroganoff, and spaghetti and meatballs, we wouldn't always want to tune in for the reruns. That's when she'd change things up, borrowing already-prepped components from these meals to come up with fresh new dishes. This chapter is dedicated to preserving my mom's ingenuity and time-saving, while also offering a fresh, modern update for how to put last night's leftovers to work. Here you'll find dishes that can easily be constructed out of your favorite weeknight meals, without a ton of new ingredients or effort—dishes that are so solid in their own right that you won't necessarily want to wait for leftovers to make them.

Tuna Salad Cakes

with Tartar Sauce

Tuna salad is one of those things that I can never get enough of (which tracks—my mom said she basically ate nothing but tuna for nine months when pregnant with me!), so it's not uncommon for me to make a few cans' worth to stash in the fridge and eat throughout the week over a bed of greens. The only problem is that sometimes, I'm not in the mood for tuna. But instead of feeling guilty and letting it all go to waste, I take a stroke of brilliance from crab cakes—those creamy, crispy pucks of perfection—and turn humble, inexpensive tuna salad into a dinner that not only I will love, but the rest of the family will too. You can also get creative with how you serve them, such as on a salad, in a grain bowl, or on a brioche bun with tartar sauce, lettuce, and tomato.

Eggs

Whole milk

Mayonnaise

Fresh chives or scallions

Tuna Salad Cakes

1 large egg

2 tablespoons whole milk

2 tablespoons all-purpose flour

½ teaspoon paprika

½ teaspoon mustard powder

½ teaspoon garlic powder

½ teaspoon onion powder

¼ teaspoon kosher salt

¼ teaspoon freshly ground black pepper

½ cup prepared tuna salad (see Note)

22 Ritz or other crackers, finely ground (1 cup), or 1 cup breadcrumbs

2 tablespoons finely chopped fresh chives or scallions

Vegetable oil, for frying

Tartar Sauce

⅓ cup mayonnaise

8 cornichons, minced (about ¼ cup; see Note)

2 tablespoons finely chopped fresh chives or scallions

1 garlic clove, minced

1 tablespoon fresh lemon juice (about ½ lemon)

½ teaspoon hot sauce

½ teaspoon mustard powder

¼ teaspoon kosher salt

Freshly ground black pepper

- **Make the tuna cakes:** In a medium bowl, whisk together the egg, milk, flour, paprika, mustard powder, garlic powder, onion powder, salt, and pepper. Fold in the tuna salad until evenly coated. Gently fold in the crackers and chives until just combined.

- Line a baking sheet with parchment paper. Divide the mixture into 4 even pieces and use your hands to gently form each piece into a ball. Arrange the balls on the prepared baking sheet and gently press on each to form a patty roughly 3 inches wide and ¼ inch thick. Cover the sheet with plastic wrap and refrigerate for 30 minutes or up to 4 hours.

- **While the tuna cakes chill, make the tartar sauce:** In a medium bowl, whisk together the mayonnaise, cornichons, chives, garlic, lemon juice, hot sauce, mustard powder, salt, and a couple of cracks of pepper. If serving the tuna cakes now, transfer the sauce to a serving bowl. Otherwise, store the sauce in an airtight container in the refrigerator for up to 5 days.

- In a large sauté pan or cast-iron pan over medium heat, add enough oil to come up the sides by ¼ inch. Heat until the oil shimmers or registers 320°F on a thermometer. Add the cakes, working in batches if necessary so as not to overcrowd the pan. Cook for about 4 minutes total, flipping halfway through, or until the cakes are golden brown and crispy on both sides. Transfer to a paper towel–lined plate and let rest 3 to 4 minutes to cool slightly before serving with the tartar sauce.

Note

If you don't already have prepared tuna salad on hand, you can whip up a simple version by combining canned tuna with mayo and salt and pepper to taste. Also, while I love the taste of cornichons here, you could also use chopped dill pickles.

Throwback Pickled Shrimp Canapés

One of the greatest things about buying those big bags of frozen shrimp is that you're always minutes away from having a meal pulled together. The downside, I've found, is that no matter how hard I try, I'm always left with just a handful of shrimp at the bottom of the bag. And when that happens, I know it's time to make this dish. I've always loved Southern food, and this classic preparation, where the shrimp "pickles" in a lemon juice–Old Bay brine and is served over a creamy spread, is appetizer heaven.

Fresh herbs

Fennel

Plain cream cheese

Mayonnaise

2 tablespoons plus 1 teaspoon fresh lemon juice

1 tablespoon extra-virgin olive oil

1 garlic clove, minced

1 teaspoon kosher salt

½ teaspoon Old Bay seasoning

3 tablespoons finely chopped fresh herbs, such as dill, chives, scallions, parsley, basil, or fennel fronds, plus more for serving

12 (21/25) cooked shrimp, tails removed, peeled, and deveined

¼ fennel bulb, cored and thinly sliced (about ½ cup)

½ cup (4 ounces) plain cream cheese, at room temperature

¼ cup mayonnaise

Freshly ground black pepper

12 baguette rounds, toasted; or crackers

- In a medium bowl, whisk together 2 tablespoons of the lemon juice with the olive oil, garlic, ½ teaspoon of the salt, the Old Bay, and 1½ tablespoons of the herbs. Fold in the shrimp and fennel. Let the mixture marinate in the refrigerator for at least 30 minutes, or up to overnight.

- In a small bowl, combine the cream cheese, mayonnaise, the remaining 1 teaspoon lemon juice, the remaining ½ teaspoon salt, and pepper to taste. Using a rubber spatula, press the mixture against the sides of the bowl to evenly combine until smooth. Fold in the remaining 1½ tablespoons herbs. Use immediately or store in an airtight container in the refrigerator for up to 3 days. Make sure to bring the mixture back to room temperature before using.

- Top the bread rounds or crackers with some of the cream cheese mixture, then a few slices of fennel, followed by the shrimp. Serve immediately.

Note

This recipe calls for the shrimp to be cooked first. If you already have some left over from that shrimp cocktail or peel-and-eat shrimp night, you're ahead of the game. If not, thaw your shrimp if frozen. Bring a medium pot of water to a boil, add the shrimp, and cover. Remove the pot from the heat and let the shrimp sit until they're cooked through and bright pink, 5 to 8 minutes.

Hot (Damn) Seafood Dip

with Crackers

My '70s soul loves a good hot seafood dip, and this might be the best one yet. Not only is it decadent and dunk-worthy, but it's also the perfect reincarnation of just about any leftover fish or shellfish. Don't worry, I threw in some spinach too. Because balance. Serve with plenty of Ritz crackers, crudités, potato chips, or slices of baguette.

Sour cream

Mayonnaise

Frozen spinach

Melting cheese, such as pepper Jack, low-moisture mozzarella, cheddar, or Monterey Jack

Note

You can use any melting cheese you like here instead of the pepper Jack, such as low-moisture mozzarella, cheddar, or Monterey Jack.

¾ cup (6 ounces) plain cream cheese, at room temperature

¼ cup sour cream

3 tablespoons mayonnaise

2 teaspoons garlic powder

1 teaspoon fresh lemon juice

1 teaspoon kosher salt

¼ teaspoon freshly ground black pepper

1 cup frozen spinach, thawed and excess liquid squeezed out

½ cup shredded pepper Jack cheese (see Note)

1 cup cooked seafood, such as crab, imitation krab, or whitefish

3 tablespoons grated Parmesan cheese

Ritz crackers, baguette, crudités, and/or potato chips, for serving

- Set a rack 6 to 7 inches from the broiler. Preheat the oven to 350°F.

- In a medium bowl, combine the cream cheese, sour cream, mayonnaise, garlic powder, lemon juice, salt, and pepper. Use a rubber spatula to mix the ingredients until smooth. Fold in the spinach and pepper Jack cheese, followed by the seafood.

- Spread the dip on the bottom of a 1-quart casserole dish and sprinkle the Parmesan over the top. Bake for 25 to 30 minutes, until the dip is bubbling around the edges and the Parmesan is golden brown in spots.

- Turn the broiler on low and broil the dip for 2 minutes, or until the Parmesan becomes a deep golden brown all over. Let the dip rest for a few minutes before serving with your favorite dippers.

Sausage, Beans, 'n' Greens

When I was growing up, it felt like there was barely a week that went by without us having either Campbell's Bean with Bacon soup or franks and beans. It made good sense—they were hearty, came together in no time, and everybody made all gone. I wanted to update this childhood favorite by adding some greens to freshen it up, but also giving a nod to the fact that stews are the perfect way to let leftovers shine. That could be leftover sausage, cooked beans, or any greens that you happen to have in your fridge.

Yellow onion

Fresh parsley

Low-sodium chicken stock

Note

If you don't have leftover sausage, you can substitute an already-smoked sausage like kielbasa, or you can roast raw sausage (such as sweet or hot Italian) until cooked through. Let the sausage rest for a few minutes before slicing it.

1 large bunch of any greens, such as collard greens, kale, Swiss chard, mustard greens, beet tops, or cabbage (about 10 large leaves)

1 cup dry white wine, such as pinot grigio or sauvignon blanc

1½ teaspoons kosher salt

18 cherry tomatoes

¼ cup plus 1 teaspoon extra-virgin olive oil

½ small yellow onion, finely diced (about ½ cup)

½ cup fresh parsley leaves, finely chopped, plus more for serving

6 garlic cloves, minced

2 (15-ounce) cans cannellini beans, drained and rinsed

1½ cups low-sodium chicken stock

2 cooked sausages, cut into ½-inch rounds (see Note)

½ teaspoon freshly ground black pepper

Grilled bread, for serving

Grated Parmesan cheese, for serving

- Preheat the oven to 400°F.

- If using greens, stack the leaves on top of one another on a cutting board. Trim away the bottom ½ inch of the stems. Cut the leaves into thirds lengthwise. Rotate the greens 180 degrees and cut them horizontally into 3-inch pieces. Cut any large pieces of stem into ½-inch pieces. If using cabbage, remove the core and cut into 3-inch pieces.

- In a large Dutch oven or a saucepan with a tight-fitting lid over medium-low heat, combine the greens, wine, and ½ teaspoon of the salt. Toss to coat the greens. Cover and cook, stirring every 5 minutes, until the wine has just evaporated and the greens are dark green and softened, about 20 minutes total.

- Using a paring knife, cut a small slit in the bottom of each cherry tomato (this will help release some of the tomatoes' juices as they cook). In a medium bowl, toss the tomatoes with 1 teaspoon of the olive oil. Set aside.

- In a large ovenproof sauté pan over medium-low heat, combine the remaining ¼ cup olive oil with the onion, parsley, and garlic. Cook until the garlic just begins to brown, about 6 minutes. Add the greens and any remaining liquid from the pot, plus the beans, chicken stock, and sausage. Season with the remaining 1 teaspoon salt and the pepper. Bring the mixture to a simmer, then remove the pot from the heat.

- Scatter the tomatoes over the top of the bean mixture. Transfer the pan to the oven and bake for 35 minutes, or until the sauce has thickened into a stew-like texture and the tomatoes are just bursting. Serve with grilled bread and top with parsley and grated Parmesan.

Sausage, Beans, 'n' Greens
PAGE 76

Hamburger Junior VP

I couldn't write a book with nostalgic recipes and not include an homage to the hit from my childhood, Hamburger Helper. Whenever we saw that little red box, we knew we were in for a treat. We loved it because what kid doesn't want a hearty meat sauce tossed with noodles, and my mom loved it because all she needed to do was add ground beef. This recipe flips the script—instead of buying the beef, you can use any leftovers that you might have, whether it's already cooked after taco or burger night, or sitting in your fridge or freezer waiting for an invitation to dinner. All you need to add are some veggies, pasta, and some kitchen staples for seasoning, and you have a dish that's a fresh take on the classic.

Red bell pepper

Dry white wine (such as pinot grigio or sauvignon blanc)

Sour cream

Note

You can use any type of leftover patties—beef, turkey, or even veggie burgers! You could also use any short pasta, such as farfalle, fusilli, or penne.

2 tablespoons extra-virgin olive oil

2 tablespoons unsalted butter

1 small yellow onion, diced (about 1 cup)

½ red bell pepper, stemmed, seeded, and diced (heaping ½ cup)

1 tablespoon tomato paste

2 teaspoons garlic powder

1 teaspoon chili powder

1 teaspoon kosher salt

¼ teaspoon ground cinnamon

¼ teaspoon freshly ground black pepper

½ cup dry white wine, such as pinot grigio or sauvignon blanc

2 cooked beef patties, crumbled (about 2 heaping cups; see Note)

3 cups low-sodium beef stock

2 cups medium pasta shells (see Note)

1½ cups shredded extra-sharp cheddar cheese

¼ cup sour cream

● In a large sauté pan over medium-low heat, heat the oil and butter until the butter has melted. Add the onion, bell pepper, tomato paste, garlic powder, chili powder, salt, cinnamon, and black pepper. Cook, stirring often and scraping the bottom of the pan with a wooden spoon, until the tomato paste caramelizes and the vegetables are browned, about 5 minutes.

● Pour in the wine and scrape the bottom of the pan with the spoon to release any browned bits. Add the crumbled beef patties and use your spoon to break them into even smaller pieces so they resemble ground meat. Cook until all the wine has evaporated, about 2 minutes. Pour in the beef stock and bring the mixture to a rapid simmer over medium-high heat. Stir in the pasta and reduce the heat to medium. Simmer until the pasta is al dente and the sauce has thickened to coat the pasta, about 12 minutes. Remove the pan from the heat and stir in the cheese until it melts, followed by the sour cream. Serve warm.

Something-Borrowed Bourguignon

Whether I'm making my Braised Tri Tip from my first cookbook, my Homemade Roast Beef from my blog, or a classic pot roast, I always have some leftovers. This rich, hearty stew is the perfect destination for those already-cooked stragglers because you don't need to sear the meat or braise it for an hour to develop tons of flavor. Instead, by roasting the vegetables and tomato paste in the oven first, you get the kind of complexity that no one will know started from last night's dinner. To really showcase this saucy stew, I like serving it over polenta, rice, egg noodles, or grilled bread. Or for an extra-special meal: Cheesy Grits with Herbed Browned Butter (page 151).

Fresh thyme, rosemary, and parsley

Tomato paste

Red wine

Frozen pearl onions

8 gold new potatoes (about 12 ounces total)

1 whole garlic head, top sliced off to expose the bulbs

4 large carrots, cut into 2-inch pieces

6 sprigs fresh thyme

2 sprigs fresh rosemary

2 tablespoons extra-virgin olive oil

1 tablespoon tomato paste

2 teaspoons kosher salt

½ teaspoon freshly ground black pepper

½ cup dried porcini mushrooms

1½ cups red wine (anything you'd gladly drink, so long as it's not too sweet)

2 tablespoons unsalted butter

2 tablespoons all-purpose flour

1 cup low-sodium beef stock

½ teaspoon ground allspice

1 cup frozen pearl onions, thawed

8 cups (10 to 12 ounces) roast beef cut into 1-inch cubes (see Note)

Prepared grits, polenta, rice, egg noodles, or grilled bread, for serving

2 tablespoons chopped fresh parsley, for serving

- Preheat the oven to 400°F.

- In a large high-sided, ovenproof sauté pan or a Dutch oven, combine the potatoes, garlic, carrots, thyme, rosemary, olive oil, tomato paste, 1 teaspoon of the salt, and ¼ teaspoon of the pepper. Use your hands to evenly coat the vegetables with all the other ingredients. Roast for 40 to 50 minutes, until the potatoes are tender when pierced with the tip of a paring knife and everything has browned. Transfer the vegetables to a baking sheet and set the pan aside to be used again.

- While the vegetables are roasting, add the dried mushrooms to a small bowl and cover them with cold water. Use your hands to gently clean the mushrooms, allowing any dirt to fall to the bottom of the bowl. Skim the mushrooms out and repeat this process, if necessary, until the mushrooms are clean. In another small bowl, add the mushrooms to the red wine to rehydrate them. Set aside.

Note

While beef is classic for this dish, you can sub in different leftover meats such as turkey, chicken, or even pork. Also, don't sweat an exact measure—a little more or a little less won't affect the end result.

● Heat the pan used to roast the vegetables over medium-low heat. Add the butter. When the butter has melted, stir in the flour. Continue stirring, releasing any brown bits from the bottom of the pan, until the flour is golden brown, about 2 minutes. Pour in the red wine, mushrooms, and beef stock, scraping the bottom of the pan to release any of the flour mixture. Add the roasted herbs, along with the ground allspice. Squeeze the garlic cloves out of their skins and add them to the pan.

● Bring the mixture to a boil, then reduce to a simmer. Cook until the sauce has reduced to a loose gravy-like consistency, about 10 minutes. Using a slotted spoon, remove the herbs, garlic cloves, and mushrooms and discard. Season with the remaining 1 teaspoon salt and the remaining ¼ teaspoon pepper, then stir in the pearl onions and meat. Simmer until everything is heated through, about 5 minutes. Reduce the heat to low and add the roasted carrots and potatoes. Cook until everything is warmed through, about 3 minutes. Ladle the bourguignon over grits, polenta, rice, egg noodles, or grilled bread and top with the parsley.

Something-Borrowed Bourguignon
PAGE 82

Grilled Pulled Pork Burritos

Pulled pork is like the A-plus student of leftovers. No matter what you originally made it for, it can be easily reincorporated into any number of dishes—soups or stews, enchiladas or tacos, even over the top of French fries as an updated take on poutine. (Don't knock it 'til you've tried it! Better yet, try my Cowboy Poutine recipe from my *Pull Up a Chair* cookbook!) For a completely fresh and easy take, I love wrapping it up in a soft tortilla along with vibrantly green cilantro rice and creamy pinto beans, then giving it a kiss of char from the grill or griddle.

Long-grain white rice

Fresh cilantro

Low-sodium chicken stock

Chipotle in adobo

Shredded cheese

Cilantro Rice

1¼ cups long-grain white rice

1 cup fresh cilantro stems and leaves, plus ¼ cup roughly chopped cilantro leaves for serving

1 small red onion, roughly chopped (about 1 cup)

½ cup Mexican beer or other lager-style beer

3 garlic cloves, smashed

1½ teaspoons kosher salt

2 tablespoons vegetable oil

1¼ cups low-sodium chicken stock

½ lime

Chipotle Pinto Beans

2 tablespoons vegetable oil

1 vine-ripened tomato, diced (about ¾ cup)

4 garlic cloves, minced

2 tablespoons finely chopped chipotle in adobo

2 teaspoons ground Mexican or Italian oregano leaves

2 teaspoons ground cumin

2 teaspoons kosher salt

2 (15-ounce) cans pinto beans, drained, with ½ cup liquid reserved

To Assemble

4 (10-inch) flour tortillas

2½ cups pulled pork

1 cup shredded cheese (I like pepper Jack here)

Vegetable oil

Crema, hot sauce, sour cream, guacamole, or salsa, for serving

● **Make the cilantro rice:** In a medium bowl, add the rice and cover with cold water. Drain. Repeat twice more, or until the drained water runs almost clear. On the final drain, make sure to remove as much excess water as possible. Set aside.

● In a blender, combine the cilantro stems and leaves, onion, beer, garlic, and salt. Blend until the cilantro and garlic are pureed and the mixture is bright green. Set aside.

● Heat the oil in a 2-quart saucepan with a tight-fitting lid or a Dutch oven over medium heat. Add the rice and cook, stirring often, to coat the rice in oil and evaporate any remaining water, about 2 minutes. If the rice begins to stick to the bottom of the pan, scrape the bottom with your spoon to release the rice. Add the pureed cilantro mixture and cook until the beer reduces almost completely and the raw onion flavor is cooked out, about another 2 minutes. Scrape the bottom of the pan

CONTINUES

Note

You can easily reheat pulled pork in the microwave or over low heat on the stove, stirring often. If the pork is on the dry side, add a small splash of stock or water.

again to release any rice. Add the stock, bring to a boil, reduce to a simmer, and cover. Cook over low heat until the rice is tender, about 20 minutes. Remove the pot from the heat. Let the rice sit, covered, until all the liquid has been absorbed and the rice is tender and fluffy, about 6 minutes. Remove the lid and squeeze the lime over the rice, followed by a sprinkling of the chopped cilantro. Gently fluff the rice with a fork to combine. Set aside and cover to keep warm.

- **Make the beans:** Heat the oil in a medium saucepan over medium-low heat. Add the tomato, garlic, chipotle in adobo, oregano, cumin, and salt. Cook, stirring constantly, until the tomatoes melt and become a sauce and the garlic and spices are toasted, about 6 minutes. Add the beans and their reserved liquid and cook, stirring often, until the beans are heated through and the flavors have melded, about 5 minutes. Cover and set aside.

- **Assemble the burritos:** Lay a tortilla on a clean work surface. Add a quarter of the rice (about ¾ cup) in a strip down the center, leaving about a 1-inch border on the two edges. Top the rice evenly with a quarter each of the beans, pulled pork, and cheese. Fold one of the longer sides of the tortilla up and over the filling, pulling it tight against the filling. Fold the two shorter sides of the burrito in toward the center and continue rolling the burrito to seal. Lay the burrito seam side down and repeat with the remaining 3 burritos.

- Heat a large cast-iron pan or sauté pan over medium-low heat and add enough vegetable oil to just lightly coat the pan. Add a burrito seam side down and cook, rotating every minute or so, until golden brown on all sides and the edge is sealed, 4 to 5 minutes. Repeat with the remaining burritos. Serve with sour cream, guacamole, and/or salsa, if desired.

Waldorf Chicken Salad Lettuce Cups

Roasted chicken is a mainstay in my refrigerator, whether it's left over from roasting a whole chicken (one of my favorite easy weeknight go-tos) or from grabbing a rotisserie chicken from the grocery store (the ultimate easy weeknight go-to). This salad is the perfect way to transform that leftover meat into lunch the next day, with tons of fresh herbs, a tangy sour cream–mayo dressing, and bright bits of apples and grapes. And don't forget to save the bones! You can use them for Chicken Bone Soup with Rice (page 39).

Mayonnaise

Sour cream

Fresh parsley, chives, and dill

Raw nuts such as almonds, walnuts, pistachios, or pine nuts

Note

I love fennel and its sweet, anisey flavor, which is why I include it in so many of my recipes. That also means I usually have the tops left over, which are the long, thin pieces that stick out from the bulb. Instead of discarding them, you can slice all of the tops and toss into salads for extra crunch—much like celery, which you could also use here. Additionally, this recipe calls for almonds, but you could use any other nuts.

Dressing

½ cup mayonnaise

¼ cup sour cream

2 tablespoons finely chopped fresh parsley

2 tablespoons thinly sliced fresh chives

2 tablespoons finely chopped fresh dill

Zest of 1 lemon

2 tablespoons fresh lemon juice (about 1 lemon)

¾ teaspoon kosher salt

¼ teaspoon freshly ground black pepper

Salad Cups

⅓ cup raw almonds (see Note)

3 heaping cups shredded cooked chicken

1 cup halved red or green grapes

1 small apple, such as Honeycrisp, Fuji, or Granny Smith, cored and cut into ¼-inch pieces

½ cup fennel tops (including fronds), thinly sliced (see Note)

Kosher salt and freshly ground black pepper

Leaves from 1 head Boston lettuce

- **Make the dressing:** In a medium bowl, whisk together the mayo, sour cream, parsley, chives, dill, lemon zest and juice, salt, and pepper. Set aside.

- **Make the salad cups:** Add the almonds to a small, dry skillet over medium-low heat and toast, stirring often, until the nuts become very fragrant and turn a deeper brown, 3 to 4 minutes. Let the nuts cool completely before transferring them to a cutting board and roughly chopping them.

- In a large bowl, toss together the shredded chicken, chopped almonds, grapes, apple, and fennel. Pour the dressing over the top and toss again until everything is evenly coated. Season with salt and pepper to taste. Let the salad sit for at least 10 minutes for the flavors to meld. Serve immediately, or cover and refrigerate up to 4 hours before serving. The longer the chicken salad sits, the more flavorful the chicken will become.

- To serve, lay the lettuce leaves on plates and fill each one with about ⅓ cup of chicken salad.

Surf & Turf Tacos

This is the ultimate fridge clean-out—it puts leftover fish *and* steak to work in what feels more like a complete first-time-around dish than a replay. Flaked fish gets worked into a bright, acidic escabeche-type salad with jalapeños, cilantro, and lime; while steak gets smothered in cumin-scented seared tomatoes. But the best part is that while these two preparations make for seriously good steak *or* fish tacos, you can combine them to make next-level tasty steak *and* fish tacos. Your Tuesdays just got a whole lot better!

Red onion

Jalapeños

Fresh cilantro

Chipotle in adobo

Green cabbage

Kale

Surf

½ small red onion, thinly sliced (about ½ cup)

½ small jalapeño, seeded and minced (about 1 heaping tablespoon)

2 tablespoons fresh lime juice (about 1 lime)

1 tablespoon roughly chopped fresh cilantro leaves

¼ teaspoon kosher salt, plus more to taste

¼ teaspoon freshly ground black pepper

2 cups (about 6 ounces) cooked fish, such as halibut, cod, bass, snapper, tilapia, or salmon

Turf

1 tablespoon extra-virgin olive oil

2 garlic cloves, minced

1 tablespoon finely chopped chipotle in adobo

½ teaspoon ground cumin

½ teaspoon dried oregano leaves

¼ teaspoon kosher salt, plus more to taste

8 cherry tomatoes, quartered

2 cups (about 6 ounces) thinly sliced cooked steak, at room temperature

To Assemble

1 cup thinly sliced green cabbage

1 cup thinly sliced Tuscan, curly, or red kale leaves

1 teaspoon extra-virgin olive oil

Pinch of kosher salt

8 (6- to 8-inch) yellow corn tortillas

Note

If you don't have both fish and steak, feel free to use one or the other for all the tacos. You can easily adjust the ingredients to double the number of tacos you make.

- **Make the surf:** In a small bowl, toss together the onion, jalapeño, lime juice, cilantro, salt, and pepper. Flake in the cooked fish and gently toss so the fish is evenly coated. Use immediately, or keep cold in the refrigerator for up to 30 minutes while you make the other components. Season with salt to taste before serving.

- **Make the turf:** Heat the oil in a medium sauté pan over medium-low heat. Add the garlic, chipotle in adobo, cumin, oregano, and salt. Cook, stirring occasionally to ensure the garlic doesn't burn, until the garlic is fragrant and the chipotle peppers have softened, about 2 minutes. Stir in the tomatoes and cook until they just begin to release their juices, about another 2 minutes. Add 3 tablespoons water and use a

wooden spoon to scrape up any brown bits from the bottom of the pan. Continue cooking for another minute while the sauce comes together, then remove the pot from the heat. Add the steak and season with salt to taste.

- **Assemble:** In a large bowl, toss the cabbage and kale with the olive oil and a pinch of salt. Use your hands to firmly massage the greens until they've just started to wilt.

- Warm the tortillas by wrapping them in a damp paper towel and microwaving for 20 seconds. Alternatively, you can place them over an open flame on your stovetop or on the grill, cooking until charred and softened, about 1 minute per side. Add some of the greens to each tortilla, followed by the meat and/or fish. Serve immediately.

Surf & Turf Tacos
PAGE 92

The Produce Bin

One of the biggest challenges I face in the kitchen is racing against the clock that starts the minute my veggies hit the fridge. I love using as many fresh ingredients as possible, but sometimes, no matter how many great meals I have planned that week, I feel overwhelmed by how quickly those ingredients start to lose their shine. Carrots, zucchini, and beets go soft; mushrooms get slimy; and greens start to wilt. Add the fact that my garden pumps out produce six months of the year, and I'm pretty much always behind the veggie eight ball. That's why I came up with these recipes—to give all veggies a shot at greatness before they go to the Great Compost Heap in the Sky. Whether you were overly enthusiastic at the farmers market, your kids suddenly decide they no longer like the cucumbers/bell peppers/sugar snap peas they were obsessed with the week before, or you just need a good old-fashioned fridge clean-out, these dishes will turn your produce bin into the source of your new favorite meals.

No-Frills Frittata

What I really love about this simpler-than-simple recipe is that it's the perfect home for not only the raw veggies in your crisper, which you can sauté and toss in, but also for the roasted or grilled veggies that don't get eaten the first night. These flavorful additions stand out against the versatile canvas of fluffy eggs folded with ricotta. All this frittata requires is a quick dip in a pan and a sprinkling of fresh herbs. It's perfect for breakfast, lunch, dinner, and everything in between.

Whole milk

Whole-milk ricotta

Fresh basil

8 large eggs

½ cup whole milk

1 tablespoon kosher salt

¼ teaspoon freshly ground black pepper

¼ cup extra-virgin olive oil, plus more for drizzling

2 cups roasted or grilled vegetables cut into bite-size pieces

½ cup whole-milk ricotta cheese

¼ cup fresh basil leaves, torn

2 tablespoons grated Parmesan cheese

- Place an oven rack 6 to 7 inches from the broiler. Preheat the oven to 400°F.
- In a medium bowl, whisk together the eggs, milk, salt, and pepper. Set aside.
- Heat the oil in a 9-inch nonstick, ovenproof sauté pan over medium-low heat for 2 minutes. Swirl the pan so the oil coats the bottom and edges. Pour in the egg mixture and sprinkle the veggies evenly over the top. Then dollop the ricotta in heaping tablespoons around the vegetables. Finish with the torn basil, a sprinkle of the Parmesan, and a drizzle of olive oil.
- Transfer the pan to the oven and bake until the eggs are set in the center and the edges have browned, 16 to 18 minutes. Let the frittata cool for about 5 minutes before slicing into wedges and serving.

Note

If you don't have any leftover roasted or grilled veggies, you have two choices: (1) You can make some (see page 49)! Or (2) you can quickly toss some veggies in a pan and sauté them. Add 2 tablespoons of extra-virgin olive oil to a large sauté pan over medium heat. If using potatoes, beets, carrots, or brussels sprouts (tougher, denser vegetables), add those first and cook for 6 to 8 minutes, stirring often, until they're browned and getting tender. Then add any softer veggies, like zucchini, yellow squash, mushrooms, onion, or bell peppers, and cook for another 4 to 5 minutes, until all the vegetables are tender. Season with salt and pepper and try not to nibble them all while you prepare the eggs.

Eat Your Veg Muffins

with Carrot-Oat Crumble

I often have a few carrots, zucchini, or yellow squash hanging out in my vegetable drawer by the end of the week that just didn't find their way into a meal or snack. I also know that if you put a vegetable in a muffin, a kid will eat it. I developed this recipe to be super versatile, no matter which of these veggies you have on hand. You can use a blend of all three, or just one entirely. Between the tender muffin, the crunchy crumble, and the tangy cardamom yogurt glaze, you'd never know that cleaning out the crisper (or yogurt container, for that matter) was the name of the game.

Rolled oats

Buttermilk

Whole-milk yogurt

Carrot-Oat Crumble

½ cup all-purpose flour

¼ cup grated carrot

¼ cup packed light brown sugar

¼ cup rolled oats

¼ teaspoon ground cinnamon

Pinch of kosher salt

5 tablespoons cold, unsalted butter, cut into cubes

Muffins

3 large eggs

¾ cup packed light brown sugar

½ cup buttermilk

½ cup refined or unrefined coconut oil, melted, plus more for greasing (see Note)

1 tablespoon pure vanilla paste or extract

½ teaspoon kosher salt

1 cup grated zucchini

2 ripe bananas, mashed (about ¾ cup)

1¾ cups all-purpose flour

¾ teaspoon baking powder

¾ teaspoon baking soda

Cardamom Yogurt Glaze

1 cup confectioners' sugar

2 tablespoons plain whole-milk yogurt

1 teaspoon ground cardamom

- **Make the crumble topping:** In a large bowl, stir together the flour, carrot, brown sugar, oats, cinnamon, and salt until evenly combined. Use your fingers to pinch the butter into the flour mixture until it is evenly combined and has the texture of wet sand. Refrigerate while you prepare the muffins, or up to overnight.

- **Make the muffins:** Preheat the oven to 350°F. Generously grease a 12-cup nonstick muffin tin with coconut oil. Set aside.

- In a medium bowl, whisk together the eggs, brown sugar, buttermilk, coconut oil, vanilla, and salt. Fold in the zucchini and banana until well combined.

CONTINUES

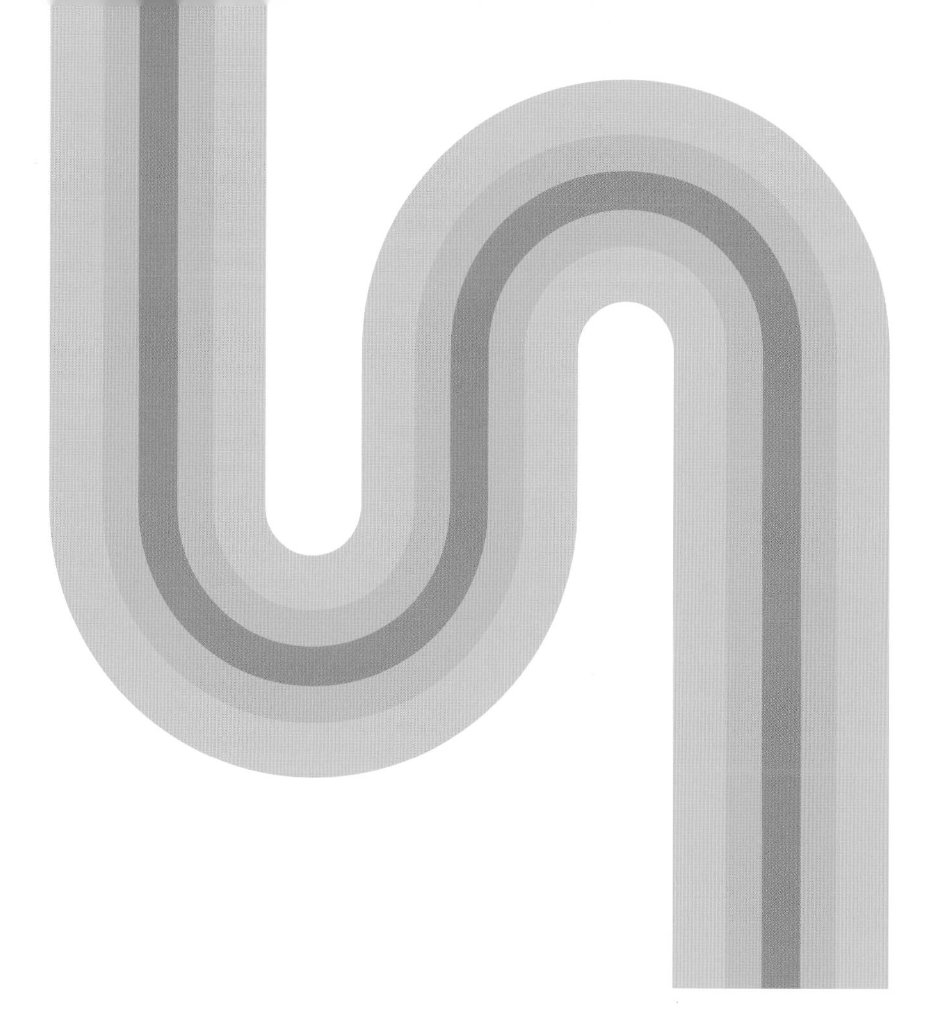

- In another large bowl, whisk together the flour, baking powder, and baking soda. Use a rubber spatula to fold the flour mixture into the egg mixture. Mix until just combined and you no longer see streaks of flour.

- Divide the batter among the muffin cups, leaving about ¼ inch at the top for the crumble. Sprinkle the crumble mixture over the top of each muffin cup. Bake for 30 minutes, or until a knife or skewer inserted into the center of a muffin comes out clean. Let the muffins cool in the pan for 15 minutes before transferring them to a cooling rack.

- **While the muffins cool, make the glaze:** In a small bowl, whisk together the confectioners' sugar, yogurt, and cardamom. Drizzle the glaze over the top of the muffins and let it set for about 10 minutes. You can store these in an airtight container at room temperature for up to 3 to 4 days.

Note

In a pinch, you could sub in vegetable oil for the coconut oil.

Veggie Ramen Salad

Any and all vegetables that you have sitting in your fridge get an instant face-lift from a quick pickling before being tossed with ramen noodles and garlic-chili dressing. The best part is that you can save the pickling liquid for another use, so it's ready the next time you want to make this dish / rescue any fading veggies. The star ingredient here is the gochujang, or Korean fermented red chili paste, which has a bold, savory flavor, manageable sweet heat, and gorgeous red color. You can find it in most grocery stores or Asian markets, and it will last just about forever in the fridge. Reach for it whenever you want to add some extra flavor to your soups, sauces, stir-fries, or eggs.

4 cups raw vegetables cut into bite-sized pieces

1½ cups plus 1 tablespoon distilled white vinegar

½ cup soy sauce

½ cup cane sugar

2 tablespoons plus ½ teaspoon kosher salt, plus more to serve

6 garlic cloves

3 tablespoons gochujang paste

1 teaspoon Chinese five spice

½ cup vegetable oil

1 teaspoon toasted sesame oil

4 (20-ounce) packets fresh ramen noodles or 4 (12-ounce) packets shelf-stable ramen noodles

4 large eggs, sunny-side up, poached, or soft-boiled, for serving (optional)

Toasted sesame seeds, for serving

- Add the vegetables to a large heatproof bowl. Set aside.

- In a medium saucepan over high heat, combine 1½ cups of the vinegar, the soy sauce, sugar, and 2 tablespoons of the salt with 2 cups water. Bring the mixture to a boil, stirring occasionally as it heats. As soon as the salt and sugar have dissolved, remove the pot from the heat and pour the pickling liquid over the vegetables. Let the vegetables sit for 6 minutes for a crunchier texture, and up to 10 minutes for slightly softer veggies. Strain the vegetables, saving the pickling liquid for other uses if desired. Refrigerate the veggies to cool completely.

- On a cutting board, mince the garlic cloves. Sprinkle the remaining ½ teaspoon salt over the minced garlic and use the side of your knife to scrape the garlic and salt into a fine paste. Place the garlic paste in a medium heatproof bowl and whisk in the gochujang paste and five spice. Set aside.

- In a small saucepan over medium heat, combine the vegetable oil and sesame oil. Heat just until you begin to see ripples (the oil should not start bubbling). Immediately pour the hot oil over the gochujang and garlic mixture. Let sit for 5 minutes to allow the garlic to cook and the oil to cool slightly. Whisk in the remaining 1 tablespoon vinegar. Continue whisking until the dressing is completely smooth. Set aside.

CONTINUES

Piquette

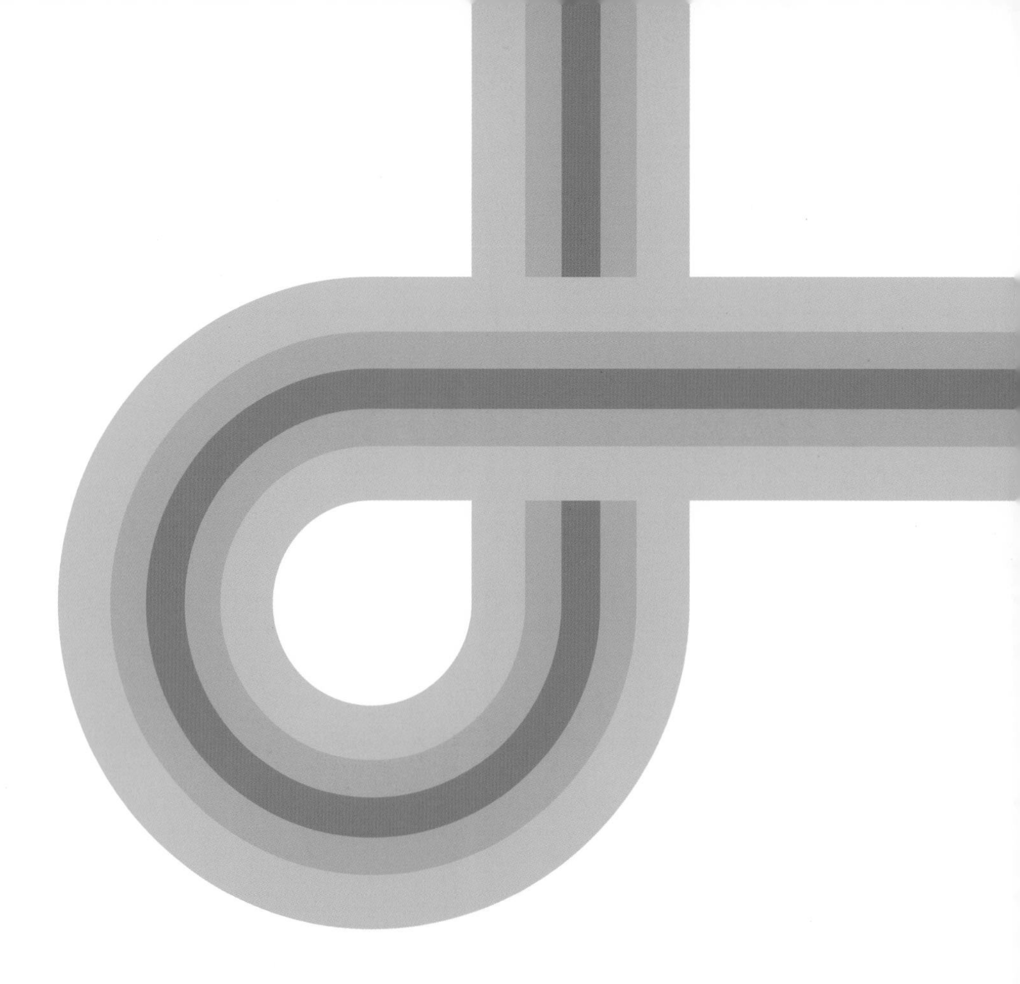

Note

This recipe would work especially well with broccoli, cauliflower, carrots, scallions (the white parts), mushrooms, radishes, and bell peppers. To save the pickling liquid, strain out any solids before letting it cool completely and storing it in the fridge in an airtight container. It will be good for up to 2 weeks.

- Bring a large pot of water to a boil. Cook the ramen noodles according to package directions. Drain the noodles in a colander and immediately run them under cold water to stop the cooking. In a large bowl, toss the noodles with the dressing. Portion the noodles among four bowls and top with the pickled vegetables and eggs, if desired. Add a pinch of salt to the eggs, sprinkle sesame seeds over the top of each bowl, and drizzle with any remaining dressing.

Savory Quinoa Porridge

with Mushrooms

Savory porridges are warm and nourishing, but they're also infinitely customizable. You can add any cooked proteins you have on hand, such as fish, tofu, or chicken; or grilled, roasted, or sautéed vegetables. I particularly love the deep, earthy flavor of mushrooms to complement the quinoa, which I bring together in a luxuriously creamy coconut milk curry. Serve this as a side dish or a main course for dinner, lunch, or breakfast with a fried or poached egg on top.

SERVES 2 AS A MAIN; 4 AS A SIDE

Roasted nuts, such as cashews, almonds, or pistachios, roughly chopped

Fresh cilantro

Yellow onion

Prepared quinoa

2 tablespoons unsalted butter

2 tablespoons vegetable oil

8 ounces mixed mushrooms, such as cremini, white button, shiitake, or oyster, cleaned, trimmed, and cut into bite-sized pieces (about 2½ cups)

2 teaspoons ground coriander

1 teaspoon ground cumin

2¼ teaspoons kosher salt, plus more to taste

¼ teaspoon freshly ground black pepper, plus more to taste

¼ cup roasted nuts, such as cashews, almonds, or pistachios, roughly chopped

¼ cup cilantro leaves and stems, roughly chopped

3 teaspoons fresh lime juice

½ medium yellow onion, diced (about ½ cup)

1 vine-ripened tomato, diced (about ½ cup)

4 garlic cloves, minced

1 tablespoon curry powder

1 (13.5-ounce) can full-fat unsweetened coconut milk, mixed well

2½ cups cooked quinoa

- In a large sauté pan over medium heat, melt 1 tablespoon of the butter with 1 tablespoon of the oil. Add the mushrooms, coriander, cumin, ½ teaspoon of the salt, and the pepper. Toss to evenly coat the mushrooms. Cook, stirring occasionally, until the pan is dry and the mushrooms are deeply browned and crispy, 10 to 12 minutes. Transfer to a plate and set aside. Do not wipe out the pan.
- In a medium bowl, toss together the nuts, cilantro, 2 teaspoons of the lime juice, ¼ teaspoon of the salt, and black pepper. Set aside.
- In the same sauté pan, combine the remaining 1 tablespoon butter and 1 tablespoon oil over medium heat. When the butter has melted, add the onion, tomato, garlic, curry powder, and 1½ teaspoons salt. Cook, stirring often, until the tomato has almost completely broken down, about 4 minutes. Add ½ cup water and use a wooden spoon to scrape up any brown bits from the bottom of the pan. Cook until the water has almost completely evaporated and the sauce is thick, about 5 minutes. Stir in another ½ cup water and the coconut milk. Bring the mixture to a boil and cook until the sauce is reduced by half and coats the back of a spoon, about 12 minutes.
- Fold in quinoa, half of the mushrooms, and 1 teaspoon lime juice. Season with salt to taste and portion among bowls. Top with the remaining mushrooms and the cilantro and nut mixture. Serve immediately.

Note

This would also be delicious with cauliflower, broccoli, zucchini, or yellow squash.

Where's the Beet Patty Melts

This recipe is tailor-made for those winter months when there's barely anything fresh to cook with besides root vegetables, especially those big softball-sized beets. For the first few weeks, I get so excited to make all things earthy and beet-y. But after that, it's not unusual for there to be at least one big guy left knocking around in the fridge and going soft. I decided to take matters into my own hands and come up with a dish that not only puts that one lone beet to work, but also transforms it into something so delectable that I can't help but get excited to make it over and over again.

Rolled oats

Low-sodium vegetable stock

Mayonnaise

½ cup rolled oats

½ cup low-sodium vegetable stock

1 large beet, cooked, peeled, and cut into 1-inch pieces (about 1 heaping cup)

1 cup canned chickpeas, drained and rinsed

1 teaspoon soy sauce

1¼ teaspoons kosher salt

¼ teaspoon freshly ground black pepper, plus more to taste

2 tablespoons unsalted butter

2 tablespoons extra-virgin olive oil

1 medium yellow onion, diced (about 1 cup)

8 slices cheddar cheese (mild, sharp, or extra-sharp)

8 slices rye bread

¼ cup mayonnaise

½ cup Thousand Island Dressing (page 169) or store-bought

● Line a baking sheet with parchment paper and set aside. Add the oats to a medium bowl and set aside.

● In a medium microwave-safe bowl or small saucepan over medium-high heat, heat the vegetable stock until just steaming, 1 minute in the microwave, 2 minutes on the stove. Pour the hot stock over the rolled oats and let them soak until most of the stock has been absorbed by the oats, 10 to 12 minutes. Drain off any liquid that hasn't been absorbed and set aside.

● In the bowl of a food processor, combine the oats, beet, chickpeas, soy sauce, 1 teaspoon of the salt, and the pepper. Pulse until the mixture is finely ground, evenly incorporated, and has just started to form a ball. Divide the mixture into 4 pieces and form them into ½-inch-thick patties. Place the patties on the prepared baking sheet, cover with plastic wrap, and refrigerate for at least 30 minutes or up to overnight.

● In a medium sauté pan over medium-low heat, combine the butter and 1 tablespoon of the oil. When the butter has melted, add the onions and the remaining ¼ teaspoon salt. Cook, stirring occasionally, until the onions have softened and caramelized, about 12 minutes. Add ¼ cup water, scraping the bottom of the pan with a wooden spoon to release any brown bits stuck to the bottom. Cook until all the water has evaporated, about 4 more minutes. Transfer the onions to a bowl and set aside.

● Heat the remaining 1 tablespoon oil in a large nonstick sauté pan or griddle pan over medium-low heat. Working in batches so as not to overcrowd the pan, add the beet patties and use a spatula to gently flatten them to ¼-inch thickness. Cook until browned on one side, about 2 minutes. Flip each patty and top with 2 slices of cheese. Cook to sear the bottom and mostly melt the cheese, about another 2 minutes. Transfer to a plate and repeat with the remaining patties.

● Spread each slice of the bread with ½ tablespoon of mayonnaise. Heat the same skillet or griddle pan over medium-low heat. Add the bread, mayo side down. Top each slice with 1 tablespoon of dressing, followed by a patty, a quarter of the caramelized onions, and another tablespoon of the dressing. Top with another slice of bread, mayo side up, and cook until the bread is deeply golden brown and crispy on each side and the sandwich is warmed through, about 2 minutes per side. Serve hot.

Where's the Beet Patty Melts
PAGE 110

All-the-Veggies Shakshuka

Shakshuka is a North African dish that features eggs poached in a pepper-tomato sauce made fragrant with spices like cumin and paprika. Aside from simmering the sauce into a thick, rich base for the eggs and sprinkling some tangy goat cheese on top, there's not much work required, and yet the layers of flavor make it seem like it took hours. I also love my version of this dish because the sauce is the perfect place to cook down any number of vegetables. This recipe calls for eggplant, but you could also toss in zucchini or mushrooms. Serve with plenty of pita for sopping up all the sauce and you have an easy meal that can be served any time of day.

Tomato paste

Prepared or store-bought tomato sauce

Goat cheese

Fresh parsley or cilantro

- 5 tablespoons extra-virgin olive oil
- 1 large red bell pepper, stemmed, seeded, and cut into large planks (about 1 heaping cup)
- 1 small or ½ large eggplant, cut into ½-inch-thick rounds
- 1½ teaspoons kosher salt, plus more to taste
- 4 garlic cloves, unpeeled
- 1 large red onion, thinly sliced (about 1½ cups)
- 1½ teaspoons smoked paprika
- 1 teaspoon ground cumin
- ½ to 1 teaspoon red pepper flakes, depending on how spicy you want to go (optional)
- ¼ teaspoon freshly ground black pepper, plus more to taste
- 2 teaspoons tomato paste
- 2 cups prepared or store-bought tomato sauce
- 4 large eggs
- ¼ cup plain or herbed goat cheese
- Chopped fresh parsley or cilantro, for serving
- Pita bread toasted with olive oil and za'atar (see Note on page 15)

- Place an oven rack 6 to 7 inches from the broiler. Preheat the oven to 425°F.

- Drizzle 2 tablespoons of the olive oil over a baking sheet. Toss the bell pepper and eggplant slices in the oil until coated. Sprinkle with ½ teaspoon of the salt and toss again. Arrange the vegetables in a single layer, add the garlic, and roast until the vegetables are soft and browned, about 20 minutes. Remove the vegetables and reduce the oven temperature to 375°F.

- When cool enough to handle, squeeze the garlic cloves out of their skins and smash the cloves into a fine paste. Roughly chop the vegetables. Set aside.

● Heat the remaining 3 tablespoons olive oil in a 9- or 10-inch high-sided sauté pan over medium heat. Add the onion and cook, stirring often, until it has softened and caramelized, 16 to 18 minutes. Add the paprika, cumin, red pepper flakes, the remaining 1 teaspoon salt, and the black pepper and stir to combine well. Stir in the roasted vegetables and tomato paste to coat everything in the pan. Cook until the eggplant begins to break down and a thick vegetable paste forms, about 5 minutes.

● Add the tomato sauce and ½ cup water, using a wooden spoon to scrape up any browned bits from the bottom of the pan. Bring the mixture to a simmer and reduce the heat to low. Gently simmer for 5 to 6 minutes, until the sauce thickens and a trail is left behind your spoon when stirring. Remove the pan from the heat.

● Use your spoon to create 4 wells in the sauce. Crack an egg into a bowl, then pour the egg into one of the wells. Repeat with the remaining eggs. Season each egg with salt and pepper. Crumble the cheese over the top of the sauce and transfer the pan to the oven. Bake until the egg whites are set and the yolks are still runny, 10 to 12 minutes. Garnish with herbs and serve immediately with toasted pita bread.

All-the-Veggies Shakshuka
PAGE 114

Any-Season Savory Tart

I call this my any-season tart because you can make a batch of this flaky, Parmesan-flecked dough and top it with any filling that works with what's in season. I'll add sliced heirloom tomatoes and cherry tomatoes with thyme and fontina in the summer, asparagus and fennel with Parm in the spring, and carrots and brussels sprouts with Gruyère in the fall. This caramelized mixed-onion tart is a favorite combo in the winter. Consider this your permission to get creative!

Fresh thyme

Fontina cheese

Crust

2½ cups all-purpose flour

2 sticks (1 cup) cold unsalted butter, cut into ½-inch cubes

¼ cup finely grated Parmesan cheese

Pinch of kosher salt

½ cup ice water

To Assemble

2 tablespoons extra-virgin olive oil

6 large shallots, sliced into ¼-inch rings without separating the rings (about 1½ cups)

6 cipollini onions, peeled and kept whole

12 red pearl onions, peeled and kept whole

¾ teaspoon kosher salt, plus more for sprinkling

¼ teaspoon freshly ground black pepper

1 cup dry sherry

1 tablespoon fresh thyme leaves

2 tablespoons unsalted butter, cut into ¼-inch cubes

All-purpose flour, for dusting

½ cup shredded fontina cheese

- **Make the crust:** In the bowl of a food processor, combine the flour, butter, Parmesan, and salt. Pulse a few times until the butter is the size of peas. Add the ice water a few tablespoons at a time, pulsing until the dough just comes together in a ball. Form the dough into a disk, wrap it in plastic wrap, and refrigerate for at least 30 minutes or overnight. Let the dough sit at room temperature for 30 minutes before rolling it out. (This is approximately the amount of time it takes to prep and cook the filling.)

- **Assemble:** Preheat the oven to 425°F. Line a baking sheet with parchment paper and set aside.

- Heat 1 tablespoon of the oil in a large sauté pan over medium heat. Add the shallots, cipollini onions, pearl onions, salt, and pepper. Cook while gently shaking the pan (not stirring, as that will break up the shallot rings) every minute or so, until the onions are softened but haven't started to brown, about 5 minutes. Add the sherry and use a wooden spoon to scrape up any brown bits from the bottom of the pan. Sprinkle in the thyme and bring the mixture to a boil. Cook at a boil until the onions are tender and the sherry has reduced to about ¼ cup, 10 to 12 minutes. Remove the pan from the heat. Scatter the butter over the top and let it melt into the onions.

● On a lightly floured surface, roll the dough into a 15-inch round. Transfer the dough to the prepared baking sheet. Brush the dough with the remaining 1 tablespoon olive oil and add a sprinkle of salt. Top the dough with the fontina, leaving at least a 1½-inch border around the edges. Spread the onion mixture over the cheese and drizzle any sauce that remains in the pan over the onions. Fold the edges of the dough toward the middle of the tart to create a 2-inch border. It will look rustic, and that's what you're going for! Bake for 30 to 35 minutes, until the tart's crust is golden brown on the edges and bottom. Let the tart cool slightly before slicing and serving.

(I'm So) Stuffed Shells

Of all the things to love about this recipe—besides the fact that everybody likes cheesy, saucy stuffed jumbo pasta, that prep takes virtually no time, and that this is the perfect make-ahead dinner—is that it's the ideal home for the last cup or so of marinara sauce in the jar or last week's meat sauce, plus the dregs of any frozen veggies you have sitting in the freezer. I call for spinach here, but you could also toss in peas, cubed squash, or riced cauliflower.

Whole-milk ricotta cheese

Eggs

Frozen spinach

Fresh herbs

Prepared tomato sauce

Low-moisture mozzarella cheese

16 jumbo pasta shells

1 cup whole-milk ricotta cheese

1 large egg

½ cup grated Parmesan cheese

Zest of 1 lemon

2 garlic cloves, minced

¼ to ½ teaspoon red pepper flakes, depending on how spicy you want to go (optional)

1½ teaspoons kosher salt

¼ teaspoon freshly ground black pepper

¼ cup defrosted frozen chopped spinach, excess moisture squeezed out

¼ cup chopped fresh herbs, such as parsley or basil

1½ cups prepared or store-bought tomato sauce, with or without meat

½ cup shredded low-moisture mozzarella cheese

1 tablespoon extra-virgin olive oil

- Place the top rack 6 to 7 inches from the broiler. Preheat the oven to 375°F.

- Bring a large pot of salted water to a boil. Stir in the pasta shells and cook for 2 minutes less than the package directions, or until the pasta is slightly less cooked than al dente. Drain the shells and run them under cold water to stop them from cooking more. Set aside.

- In a medium bowl, stir together the ricotta, egg, ¼ cup of the Parmesan, the lemon zest, garlic, red pepper flakes (if using), salt, and black pepper until evenly combined. Add the spinach and 2 tablespoons of the herbs and mix well. Divide the mixture among the shells.

- Add 1 cup of the tomato sauce to the bottom of an 8 x 8-inch baking dish. Arrange the shells, filling side up, so they fill the pan in an even layer. Top the shells with the remaining ½ cup sauce. Sprinkle the mozzarella over the sauce, followed by the remaining 2 tablespoons herbs and the remaining ¼ cup Parmesan.

- Tear off a piece of foil large enough to cover the baking dish. Brush one side of the foil with the oil and then place the foil, oil side down, over the shells. Bake for 30 minutes. Remove the baking dish from the oven and switch the oven to the low broil setting. Remove the foil and broil the shells until the cheese is golden brown on top, 4 to 5 minutes. Let rest 5 to 10 minutes before serving.

Creamy Broccoli Soup

with Cheddar "Crackers"

When served this silky, vibrant green soup, no one would guess that it was the result of an ingredient that would otherwise be left for compost: broccoli stems. Especially when garnished with golden, crispy cheddar cheese "crackers." And your kids will never figure out that the recipe calls for potatoes instead of loads of cream to give the soup its decadently thick consistency, or that there's a whole bunch of spinach for good green measure. That's a whole lot of winning!

Sour cream

Fresh chives

2 large stalks broccoli, tough ends removed, cut into ½-inch rounds (about 1½ cups)

4 large garlic cloves, unpeeled

1 tablespoon extra-virgin olive oil

1⅓ cups shredded extra-sharp cheddar cheese

4 cups low-sodium vegetable stock

1 medium Yukon Gold or russet potato (8 ounces), scrubbed and cut into 1-inch pieces (about 1 cup; see Note)

3 cups packed baby spinach leaves

1 teaspoon kosher salt, plus more to taste

¼ teaspoon freshly ground black pepper, plus more to taste

½ cup sour cream

Sliced fresh chives, for serving (optional)

- Preheat the oven to 400°F.

- On a baking sheet, toss together the broccoli, garlic, and olive oil. Roast for 15 minutes; remove the garlic, and set aside. Flip the broccoli stems and continue roasting for an additional 15 minutes, or until browned and tender. Remove the broccoli from the oven and leave the oven on.

- Line a second baking sheet with parchment paper. Divide the cheese into 4 even mounds, about ⅓ cup per mound. Use your fingers to spread the cheese into even 3-inch rounds. Bake until the cheese is melted and brown around the edges, about 8 minutes. Set aside to cool; the cheese will crisp into "crackers" as it sits.

- In a large pot or Dutch oven over high heat, combine the stock and potatoes with 2 cups water. Bring to a boil, then reduce to a simmer over medium-low heat. Cook until the potatoes are cooked through and tender, about 10 minutes. Use a slotted spoon to transfer the potatoes to a bowl, leaving the stock in the pot.

- Squeeze the roasted garlic cloves out of their skins. In a blender, combine the garlic, spinach, broccoli, and potatoes. Add about 2 cups of the stock, just enough to help the vegetables blend together. Remove the top cap from the blender and place a clean towel over the opening. This will help some of the steam escape as the soup blends but prevent any splattering. Starting on the lowest setting, begin blending the soup until smooth. Gradually increase the speed until the soup is completely smooth. Add the soup back into the pot with the stock, plus the salt and pepper. Taste and adjust the seasoning as needed.

● Add the sour cream to a small bowl. Ladle in 1 cup of the hot soup and whisk immediately to combine. This will help keep the sour cream from curdling when added back to the soup. Stir the sour cream mixture into the soup. Bring the soup to a gentle simmer just to heat it through. Remove the pot from the heat and serve immediately with the cheddar crackers and a sprinkling of chives, if using.

Note

Any size or type of potato will work here, whether it's a large white potato or a handful of new or fingerling potatoes.

Butternut Squash Quesadillas

One of the vegetables my kids will never say no to is butternut squash, which means that I'm always looking for new ways to use it. Most often I'm dicing one up and throwing it in the oven to roast, and while they usually descend on the baking sheet the minute the squash is cool enough to handle, there's always a cup or two that doesn't get inhaled. That's when I fold the leftovers into a smoky roasted tomato mixture that gets topped with plenty of cheese, wrapped in a tortilla, and griddled. Served with a dollop of lime sour cream, this dish does justice to the amazing Mexican restaurants in Los Angeles that I was inspired by.

Sour cream

Red onion

Fresh cilantro

Lime Sour Cream

½ cup sour cream

2 teaspoons fresh lime juice

½ teaspoon kosher salt

Quesadillas

12 halved cherry tomatoes (about 1 cup)

½ medium red onion, peeled, trimmed, and halved

2 large garlic cloves, unpeeled

1 to 2 chipotles in adobo, strained from their liquid and minced (1 to 2 tablespoons; see Note)

1 tablespoon vegetable oil, plus more for greasing

1 teaspoon kosher salt, plus more to taste

½ teaspoon dried oregano leaves

½ teaspoon ground cumin

1½ cups cooked butternut squash cut into ½-inch pieces

2 tablespoons roughly chopped fresh cilantro leaves

4 (10-inch) flour tortillas

2 cups shredded melting cheese, such as a Mexican blend, cheddar, Monterey Jack, pepper Jack, or mozzarella

Roasted pepitas, pomegranate seeds, cilantro leaves, guacamole, and/or salsa, for serving (optional)

- **Make the lime sour cream:** In a small bowl, whisk together the sour cream, lime juice, salt, and 1 tablespoon water. This can be stored in an airtight container for up to 5 days.

- **Make the quesadillas:** Place an oven rack 6 to 7 inches from the broiler. Preheat the oven on the low broil setting.

- On a large baking sheet, combine the tomatoes, onion, garlic, chipotle, oil, salt, oregano, and cumin. Toss everything until the vegetables are well coated. Broil for about 6 minutes, or until the garlic is tender, the tomatoes are charred, and the onions have softened. Let cool slightly.

- When cool enough to handle, remove the garlic cloves from their skins. Transfer the garlic and onion to a cutting board and roughly chop. Transfer the mixture to a large bowl and add the roasted tomatoes, squash, and cilantro. Season with more salt, if needed.

- Lay a tortilla on a clean work surface. Sprinkle ¼ cup of the cheese over half of the tortilla. Top the cheese with ¼ of the squash mixture, followed by another ¼ cup of cheese. Fold the half of the tortilla with no toppings over the filling to create a half-moon. Repeat with the remaining tortillas.

- Heat a large cast-iron pan or griddle pan over medium-low heat for about 2 minutes. Add enough oil to coat the bottom and cook 1 quesadilla at a time until the tortilla is crispy and the cheese has melted, about 3 minutes per side. Repeat with the remaining quesadillas.

- Cut the quesadillas into wedges, if desired. Serve with the lime sour cream and/or desired toppings.

Note

You can substitute any other type of roasted winter squash in this recipe. Alternatively, you could use defrosted frozen squash. You can also play with the spice factor: If you don't love spice, use 1 chipotle in adobo. If it's your thing, add 2. Last, if you want to make these for company and keep them warm as you make the batch, you can hold them in a 200°F oven.

Butternut Squash Quesadillas
PAGE 124

Rescue-Those-Berries Preserves

We've been talking about leftover veggies up until this point, but that doesn't mean fruit shouldn't get our attention too. Especially berries, which sometimes seem to have about a 5-minute life span, even when you've gotten them at peak season from the farmers market. Instead of feeling like you need to eat them all at once (which we do, with no regrets), you could also turn them into this simple spread. The perk is that you can enjoy the fresh berry flavor for a lot longer, especially dolloped over Baked French Toast (page 2); alongside Saucy Swedish Meatballs (page 24); stirred into a Pink Lady (page 177); or as a Sour Cream Doughnut (page 180) glaze.

MAKES 2 CUPS

2 cups mixed fresh berries

2 tablespoons fresh lemon juice (about 1 lemon)

1½ cups cane sugar

● In a small saucepan over medium heat, combine the berries and lemon juice. Lightly mash the berries with a potato masher or slotted spoon to break them down into smaller pieces and release some of their juice. Continue cooking until the berries begin to soften and their juices come to a boil, about 3 minutes. Stir in the sugar and bring the mixture back to a simmer. Reduce the heat to low to maintain a gentle simmer and continue cooking until the berries are extremely soft and the syrup coats the back of the spoon, about 10 minutes. Remove the pan from the heat and let cool completely before storing in an airtight container in the refrigerator for up to 2 weeks.

Aunt Jenny's Sweet Potato Cake Roll

My Aunt Jenny is known for the pumpkin roll that she makes for the holidays every year. It's the ultimate crowd-pleaser with its impressive swirl of pumpkin-infused cake layered with a cream cheese filling. So when I found myself with extra roasted sweet potatoes after batch cooking them for the week's meals, my mind naturally went to Aunt Jenny's cake. I swapped out the pumpkin for the sweet potato and here you have it—a seasonal dessert that is as gorgeous as it is practical.

Whole milk

Sour cream

Nonstick cooking spray

1 cup roasted and peeled sweet potato

1½ cups whole milk

1 teaspoon pumpkin pie spice

1 tablespoon pure vanilla paste or extract

6 large eggs, yolks and whites separated

1 stick (8 tablespoons) unsalted butter, melted

1 cup all-purpose flour

1 tablespoon fresh lemon juice (about ½ lemon)

½ cup granulated sugar

½ cup apricot, orange, or lemon preserves

8 ounces plain cream cheese, at room temperature

¼ cup sour cream

½ cup confectioners' sugar, plus more for dusting

- Preheat the oven to 350°F. Spray a 9 x 13-inch sheet tray with nonstick spray. Line the tray with parchment paper, leaving about an inch of overhang on each side. Spray the parchment with more nonstick spray and set aside.

- In a blender, combine the sweet potato, milk, pumpkin pie spice, and vanilla and blend until smooth.

- Add the egg yolks to a large bowl. Whisk while streaming in the melted butter and continue whisking until well combined. Whisk in the pureed sweet potato mixture. Sift in the flour and whisk until you no longer see streaks of flour and the batter is smooth. Set aside.

- In the bowl of a stand mixer fitted with the whisk attachment, whip the egg whites and lemon juice on medium-high speed until the egg whites are foamy and thickened, about 2 minutes. With the mixer running, slowly stream in the granulated sugar. Continue whisking until the egg whites hold soft peaks and are glossy, 4 to 5 minutes more.

CONTINUES

- Working in batches, gently fold the whipped egg whites into the sweet potato mixture until just combined. Make sure not to overmix the batter or you will deflate the egg whites and your cake will be dense. Pour the batter into the prepared pan and use a spatula to gently spread it to the edges. Give the pan a gentle shake to encourage the batter to sit evenly in the pan.

- Bake until the top of the cake is golden brown, no longer sticky to the touch, and a knife or skewer inserted into the center comes out clean, about 35 minutes. Cool for 15 minutes, until the cake has deflated slightly and set. While still slightly warm, evenly spread the apricot preserves over the cake. Let the cake completely cool for another 15 to 20 minutes.

- In a stand mixer fitted with the paddle attachment, cream together the cream cheese, sour cream, and confectioners' sugar until evenly combined and smooth, about 2 minutes.

- Spread the cream cheese filling evenly over the top of the preserves, leaving a 1-inch border on all sides of the cake. Supporting the cake on both ends with your hands, gently lift the longer edge of the cake using the parchment paper "handles."

- Gently roll the cake about 2 inches over the top. Continue carefully rolling the cake over the filling, peeling away the parchment paper as you go. When you finish, turn the cake seam side down to seal it. Dust the cake with confectioners' sugar and slice into rounds to serve. Any leftover cake can be wrapped in plastic and refrigerated for 2 to 3 days.

Note

Roasted winter squash also works well for this recipe. And if you don't have enough leftover roasted squash or sweet potato to fill 1 cup, you can supplement with canned.

Cheese Bits

Whether it's sliced options for sandwiches, shredded varieties for quesadillas and pizzas, leftover charcuterie board offerings, or the stray brick or two that just sounded good when I was shopping, I pretty much always have more cheese than I know what to do with. Short of snacking on it all day long, I like using these options as jumping-off points for meals—after all, cheese is so often the selling point of a dish. Whether it's whipped into spreads, melted over bread, swirled into pasta, or folded into butter—it's safe to say that pretty much everything is better with cheese. So when you're staring into your own cheese drawer (or entire chest, if your fridge is like mine), start to see inspiration for what to make next. These recipes will get you the rest of the way.

Marinated Stuffed Olives

Whenever I have people over for dinner or cocktails, I always like to have a few nibbles set out beforehand. And because I believe in not overcomplicating things, I usually put together a mix of store-bought and homemade offerings. One of my go-to homemade additions is cheese-stuffed olives marinated in garlic- and chili-infused oil and balsamic vinegar. I can't begin to tell you how impressed people are every time I serve them, and yet they couldn't be simpler to make. But the best part is that you can most likely make this dish out of things you already have in the fridge and pantry, including any soft, fresh cheese such as feta, ricotta, goat, or mascarpone. Just don't forget to save the olive brine for Squeaky Clean Martinis (page 222)!

¼ cup extra-virgin olive oil

4 garlic cloves, thinly sliced

1 teaspoon red pepper flakes

1 teaspoon coriander seeds

¾ teaspoon kosher salt

2 tablespoons torn fresh mint leaves

1 tablespoon aged balsamic vinegar (see Notes)

¼ cup drained jarred pimentos, chopped into a coarse paste

1½ cups pitted green olives, drained

½ cup fresh cheese, such as goat, feta, ricotta, or mascarpone

● In a small sauté pan over medium-low heat, combine the oil, garlic, red pepper flakes, coriander, and salt. Slowly bring the mixture to a simmer and cook, while gently stirring, until the garlic is golden, about 5 minutes. Transfer the mixture to a medium bowl and stir in the mint and balsamic vinegar. Add the pimento paste and let the oil cool completely, about 15 minutes.

● Use a teaspoon or offset spatula to stuff the olives with the cheese. Add the stuffed olives to the marinade and toss to coat. Refrigerate the olives for at least 1 hour, or store them in an airtight container for up to 1 week. The longer the olives marinate, the more flavor they will take on.

Notes

I call for "aged" balsamic vinegar in this recipe, which is a little bit redundant because technically *all* the balsamic vinegar that you see at the grocery store is aged (a minimum of 12 years). But if you can find one that's 18 to 25 years old, you'll see that the sharpness mellows, bringing out a natural sweetness instead. The consistency also gets thicker and more syrupy, which gives the marinade a little extra body. But this recipe would also be delicious with whatever kind of balsamic you have in your pantry or can find at your local store.

Also, I encourage you to use this marinade, without the olives, for meats or seafood; or you could drizzle it over just about anything—whipped feta, bruschetta, eggs, and sandwiches.

All-the-Cheeses Spread & Fondue

This dish is based on the legendary French chef Jacques Pépin's *fromage fort*, a genius recipe that transforms random bits of leftover cheese into a rich spread. I like adding texture by also folding in things like fresh herbs, olives, or roasted peppers. Or, if I'm really feeling retro, I'll turn the whole thing into a fondue for a fun and unexpected treat.

Dry white wine (such as pinot grigio and sauvignon blanc)

Roasted peppers

Fresh herbs

8 ounces assorted cheeses, hard rinds removed (about 1½ cups)

½ cup dry white wine, such as pinot grigio or sauvignon blanc

1 large garlic clove, minced

¼ teaspoon freshly ground black pepper

Kosher salt

¼ cup diced roasted peppers, chopped olives, or fresh herbs (optional)

1 tablespoon cornstarch, plus more if needed (optional)

Baguette rounds, crackers, chips, crudités, and/or charcuterie, for serving

- In the bowl of a food processor, combine the cheeses, wine, garlic, and black pepper. Process until the mixture is evenly combined and has the texture of ricotta, about 1 minute. Season with salt to taste.

- If serving this as a spread, fold in any stir-ins you desire—such as peppers, olives, or herbs—until evenly combined. Serve immediately or store in the refrigerator in an airtight container for up to 1 day.

- If you're making a fondue, transfer the cheese mixture to a small pot over medium-low heat and stir in the cornstarch. Stir until the cheese melts completely to ensure the cornstarch doesn't create any lumps, anywhere from 4 to 8 minutes, depending on the types of cheeses you are using. Transfer the fondue to a fondue pot, if desired, to keep warm. Serve immediately with your favorite fondue dippers.

Note

If making fondue, you may need to sprinkle in more cornstarch, depending on the types of cheeses you use. If the fondue looks like it's separating, whisk in more cornstarch by the teaspoon until the fondue holds together.

All-the-Cheeses Spread & Fondue
PAGE 138

Cheese Drawer Soufflés

Just saying the word "soufflé" brings to mind effortlessly chic brunching—and it's true; nothing feels more sophisticated than these perfectly puffed, elegantly simple eggs served in individual ramekins. But what your guests don't need to know is that they require very little effort on your part and even fewer ingredients, including a sprinkling of whatever hard cheese you happen to have in your cheese drawer, which creates the perfect caramelized, salty, cheesy crust.

Whole milk

Fresh thyme

2 tablespoons unsalted butter, plus more for greasing

1 cup finely grated hard cheese, such as Parmesan, pecorino Romano, Asiago, Gruyère, Manchego, or Swiss

2 tablespoons all-purpose flour

1¼ cups whole milk

1½ teaspoons fresh or ¾ teaspoon dried thyme leaves, plus 2 sprigs fresh thyme (if using fresh herbs)

¼ teaspoon kosher salt

Freshly ground black pepper

5 large eggs

- Place an oven rack in the top third of the oven. Preheat the oven to 400°F.

- Grease four (8- to 10-ounce) ovenproof ramekins with butter. If using a very finely grated cheese like pecorino, Asiago, or Parmesan, use about 2 tablespoons to coat the ramekins. (Leave this step out if you're using a softer cheese.) Rotate each ramekin until the cheese coats all the butter. Tap out any excess cheese into the next ramekin and repeat until all the ramekins are lightly dusted with cheese. Set aside.

- Melt the butter in a medium saucepan over medium-low heat. Add the flour and cook, stirring constantly, until the mixture is a pale golden color, about 2 minutes. Whisk in the milk, thyme leaves, salt, and a few grinds of pepper. Increase the heat to medium and cook, whisking constantly, until the sauce reaches a boil and thickens to the point where you see a trail left behind by your whisk, about 3 minutes. Remove the pan from the heat and let cool for 5 to 10 minutes.

- In a medium bowl, whisk together the eggs. While continuing to whisk, pour in the cooled sauce, along with the remaining grated cheese. Divide the mixture among the four ramekins, filling each about ⅔ of the way to the top. Use kitchen shears to cut the remaining sprigs of thyme into 2-inch sections and top each ramekin with a piece.

- Place the ramekins on a baking sheet and bake for 30 minutes, or until the soufflés puff over the edges of the ramekins, the sides are a deep golden brown, and the tops are beginning to turn golden brown in spots. Serve immediately.

Mixed-Mushroom Quiche

Whether I'm making brunch or breakfast for dinner, I love a quiche. Just like an omelet, you can throw in pretty much whatever fillings you like, and it gets baked to perfection inside a flaky crust. In this case, I'm reaching for a mix of mushrooms plus any semisoft cheese that's available, even a mix of them. I'm partial to Havarti in this combination, but you could also go with Gouda, fontina, Muenster, pepper Jack, Stilton, goat, ricotta—you get the idea.

Fresh rosemary and thyme

Heavy cream

Crust

2½ cups all-purpose flour, plus more for dusting

1 tablespoon granulated sugar

¾ teaspoon kosher salt

2 sticks (1 cup) cold unsalted butter, cut into ½-inch cubes

6 tablespoons ice water

Quiche

12 ounces mixed mushrooms, such as cremini, shiitake, maitake, or oyster, roughly chopped (about 3½ cups)

1 tablespoon extra-virgin olive oil

1½ teaspoons kosher salt

2 sprigs fresh rosemary

2 sprigs fresh thyme

12 large eggs

1 cup grated semisoft cheese, such as Havarti, Gouda, fontina, or Muenster

½ cup grated Parmesan cheese

½ cup heavy cream

- **Make the crust:** In the bowl of a food processor, combine the flour, sugar, and salt and pulse a few times to combine. Add the butter and pulse again until the butter is the size of peas. Add the ice water 2 tablespoons at a time, pulsing between additions, until the dough just comes together and forms a ball. Shape the dough into a disk and wrap in plastic wrap. Refrigerate for at least 30 minutes or up to 3 days. Alternatively, you can freeze the dough for up to 6 months. If freezing, defrost the dough overnight in the refrigerator before using. For refrigerated and frozen dough, let the dough sit at room temperature for 30 minutes before rolling it out.

- **Make the quiche:** Preheat the oven to 350°F.

- On a baking sheet, toss together the mushrooms with the olive oil and ½ teaspoon of the salt until the mushrooms are well coated. Add 1 sprig of the rosemary and 1 sprig of the thyme and roast for 25 minutes, or until the mushrooms are golden brown. Set aside.

- On a lightly floured work surface, roll the pie dough into a 13-inch round. Transfer the dough to a 9½- or 10-inch deep-dish pie pan. Gently press the dough up the edges of the pan and trim away excess dough, leaving a ½-inch overhang. Crimp the pie dough along the edge to form the crust. Use a fork to prick the dough all over the

bottom. Place a piece of parchment over the dough and fill the pie with pie weights, dried beans, or rice. Place the pie on a baking sheet and bake for 30 minutes, or until the dough is a pale-yellow color. Remove the parchment and pie weights. Return the pie dough to the oven for another 10 to 15 minutes, until the dough is a light golden brown. Set aside and leave the oven on.

● Roughly chop the leaves from the remaining rosemary and thyme sprigs. In a large bowl, whisk together the chopped herbs, eggs, cheeses, heavy cream, and the remaining 1 teaspoon salt. Pour the mixture into the prepared crust (it does not need to be cooled completely) and scatter the roasted mushrooms over the top. Bake for 45 minutes, or until the egg has puffed and no longer jiggles when you gently shake the pan. Let the quiche cool slightly before slicing and serving.

Note

While there is nothing that compares to flaky, buttery homemade quiche crust, and it is simple to prepare and can be made in advance, consider this my blessing for you to use store-bought instead. The quiche will still be delicious! Just make sure you're buying dough and not a preformed pie shell, which may be too shallow for the filling.

Blue Cheese Buttah

One of the easiest yet most impressive ways to add flavor to a dish is with compound butter. You just need to soften a stick of butter, then fold in any number of seasonings, from fresh herbs to spices to aromatics to even edible flowers like lavender. One day, when confronted with the last crumbles of blue cheese I'd bought for a cheese board, I had the brilliant idea (if I do say so myself) to fold it into butter. And voilà, blue cheese butter was born. It's since become my favorite way to finish steaks, baked potatoes, polenta, and roasted winter vegetables.

Fresh tarragon

1 stick (8 tablespoons) unsalted butter, at room temperature

1 teaspoon lightly crushed peppercorns (see Note)

1 tablespoon fresh tarragon leaves, roughly chopped

½ teaspoon sea, truffle, pink, or smoked salt

⅓ cup crumbled blue cheese

- Cut a piece of parchment paper to measure approximately 12 x 10 inches. Spread the butter over the parchment into a roughly 5 x 8-inch rectangle. Sprinkle the butter with the peppercorns, then the tarragon, the salt, and, finally, the blue cheese. Place a piece of plastic wrap over the top and press so everything adheres to the butter. Flip the mixture over, so the plastic wrap is now on the bottom and the long side of the parchment is parallel to the counter's edge. Peel away the parchment paper and use the plastic wrap to help roll the compound butter into a log, pulling back the plastic wrap after each roll so it doesn't get stuck inside the compound butter. Once the butter is shaped, cover it completely with the plastic wrap, then roll the ends of the plastic like a piece of taffy candy to tighten the cylinder of butter and to seal. Refrigerate until firm, at least 1 hour. Store the butter in the refrigerator for up to 2 weeks, or add it to a freezer-safe zip-top bag and freeze for up to 3 months.

Note

Feel free to have fun with the peppercorns here, which can add pretty colors in addition to a variety of flavors. Try pink, green, black, white, or a mixture of all the above. Or, as with any other recipe here, use whatever you have handy!

Blue Cheese Buttah

PAGE 146

Cheesy Grits

with Herbed Browned Butter

A big potful of creamy grits is a staple on our dinner table because it just doesn't get any easier or more versatile. You can throw in just about any melty cheese you have on hand—Colby, Havarti, fontina, Monterey Jack, Muenster, provolone, Swiss, smoked Gouda, goat, Brie—and it will instantly transform the simple combination of cornmeal and milk into rich, gooey heaven.

1½ cups whole milk

2¼ teaspoons kosher salt

1 cup yellow or white corn grits

1½ cups shredded cheddar cheese or other melting cheese

4 tablespoons unsalted butter

Freshly ground black pepper

1 large garlic clove, thinly sliced

¼ cup fresh herbs, such as parsley, sage, and/or thyme, roughly chopped

Note

You can make this recipe with pretty much any kind of grits or cornmeal—stone-ground, quick-cooking, instant, yellow, or white. The amount of time the grits will need to cook will depend on the type you buy, so be sure to reference the packaging for the recommended cook time.

- In a large pot or Dutch oven over medium-high heat, combine the milk and 2 teaspoons of the salt with 2½ cups water. Bring to a boil, then reduce to a gentle simmer over low heat. Slowly stream in the grits while whisking. Continue to gently simmer, stirring often to prevent the grits from sticking to the bottom or spitting too much, until the grits are tender and the mixture is creamy, 10 to 12 minutes. Remove the pot from the heat and stir in the shredded cheese to melt. Cover the grits to keep warm.

- In a small sauté pan over medium-low heat, melt the butter with the remaining ¼ teaspoon salt and a few grinds of pepper. Add the garlic and cook, while gently and constantly swirling the pan, until the butter browns and the garlic is toasted, about 3 minutes. Remove the pan from the heat. Carefully tilt the pan slightly so the butter pools on one side. Add the herbs where there is no butter, then slowly and gently lower the pan back onto a flat surface. Let the herbs fry gently in the butter as it cools.

- Portion the grits into four bowls and spoon some of the herbed butter over the top. Serve immediately.

Parmesan Cream Scalloped Potatoes

If I could give you one great cooking tip, it would be to never, ever throw away the rind from your finished Parmesan cheese. It has the ability to turn the volume up on soups, stocks, and sauces with that unique salty, savory flavor of Parmesan—and without any added cost or effort. Here we're baking thinly sliced potatoes in a bath of Parm-rind-infused cream sauce to make the ultimate side dish. It would be right at home served alongside pan-seared steaks or roasted chicken on a weekday or as part of a spread for a special occasion or holiday.

Fresh thyme

Parmesan Cream

4 cups heavy cream

2 or 3 (3- to 4-inch) Parmesan cheese rinds

½ large yellow or red onion, quartered

6 whole allspice berries

4 sprigs fresh thyme

1 dried or fresh bay leaf

2 teaspoons kosher salt

Freshly ground black pepper

Scalloped Potatoes

1 tablespoon unsalted butter

3 large Yukon Gold potatoes (1½ pounds), peeled and cut into ⅛-inch-thick slices

1 tablespoon fresh thyme leaves

Freshly ground black pepper

Note

To build your collection of Parmesan rinds, toss them into a freezer-safe zip-top bag and store them in the freezer until you're ready to use them.

- **Make the Parmesan cream:** In a large saucepot or Dutch oven over medium heat, combine the heavy cream, Parmesan rinds, onion, allspice, thyme, and bay leaf. Bring the mixture to a boil, then reduce to a simmer over medium-low heat. Cook, stirring occasionally, until the sauce has thickened to the consistency of an alfredo sauce, about 30 minutes. Immediately strain the sauce through a fine-mesh sieve into a medium bowl. Add the salt and season with black pepper to taste. Set aside while you make the potatoes.

- **Make the potatoes:** Preheat the oven to 350°F.

- Melt the butter in an 8- or 9-inch ovenproof sauté pan over medium-low heat. Remove the pan from the heat. Pour ½ cup of the cream sauce into the pan and use a spoon or spatula to evenly spread it across the bottom. Top the sauce with a layer of the potatoes, shingling the slices in a circle around the outer edge and then working toward the center. Top with another ½ cup of the sauce and repeat until you've used all the potatoes and sauce. (This will be about four layers of potatoes, ending with the sauce on top.) Sprinkle the thyme leaves over the top and season with a few cracks of black pepper.

- Bake for 50 minutes, or until the top is golden brown and the sauce is bubbling around the edges of the pan. Let the potatoes rest for 10 to 15 minutes to cool slightly and to set, which will make them easier to slice and serve.

Deluxe Grilled Cheese Sandwiches

with Onion Jam

There's grilled cheese and then there's *grilled cheese*. This is not your mother's Kraft Singles and Wonder Bread. Instead, I'm giving new life to all those good, melty cheeses collecting in your cheese drawer—provolone, pepper Jack, fontina, Swiss, cheddar, Brie, you get the idea—by layering them up and throwing in a little sweet-savory action with jammy onions. You could stop there, or you could give your bread a schmear of miso butter before sending everything to the griddle. Now, *that's* a sandwich.

Fresh ginger

Note

Feel free to mix and match your cheeses; just about any combination will work here. Just be sure to grate or crumble them first so they melt evenly. If you opt to not make the miso butter, feel free to use regular unsalted butter or, my other favorite grilled cheese twist, mayo.

Onion Jam

2 tablespoons vegetable oil

1 medium red onion, thinly sliced (about 1 heaping cup)

¼ cup distilled white vinegar

¼ cup packed light brown sugar

1 (½-inch) piece fresh ginger, smashed

1 star anise pod

1 cinnamon stick

½ teaspoon kosher salt

¼ teaspoon freshly ground black pepper

Miso Butter

4 tablespoons unsalted butter, at room temperature

1 tablespoon white or yellow miso

To Assemble

8 slices thick-cut sourdough bread, or any other bread you may have

1½ to 2 cups shredded melting cheese, such as provolone, pepper Jack, fontina, Swiss, cheddar, or Brie

- **Make the onion jam:** Heat the oil in a large, high-sided sauté pan or Dutch oven over medium-low heat. Add the onions and cook, stirring occasionally, until the onions are tender and beginning to brown, about 10 minutes. Add the vinegar and ¾ cup water, scraping the bottom of the pan with a wooden spoon to release any brown bits. Stir in the brown sugar, ginger, spices, salt, and pepper and increase the heat to bring the mixture to a simmer. Reduce the heat to medium-low and cook, stirring occasionally, until the liquid has evaporated and the onions are coated in a syrupy glaze, about 18 minutes. Remove the cinnamon, star anise, and ginger and discard. Transfer the jam to a medium bowl and set aside. Store any extra onion jam in an airtight container in the refrigerator for up to 1 week. Spread it on toast, stir it into soups, throw it in a baked potato, or pile it on eggs.

- **Make the miso butter:** In a small bowl, mix together the butter and miso until evenly combined. Set aside. The miso butter can also be stored in an airtight container in the refrigerator for up to 1 week.

- **Assemble:** Heat a cast-iron griddle pan over medium-low heat. Brush one side of each bread slice with miso butter. Turn 4 bread slices over and spread onion jam over the top. Top the onion jam with about ½ cup of cheese, then add the top slice of bread, miso butter side up. Transfer the sandwiches to the pan and cook until both sides are deeply golden brown, 7 to 8 minutes total. If your bread is toasted before the cheese is melted, remove the pan from the heat and cover it with a lid until the cheese melts.

Stuffed Zucchini "Subs"

I love a meatball sub, and whenever I see shredded mozzarella in my fridge, it's one of the first recipes that come to mind. But because mozzarella is pretty much a permanent fixture—we're DIY pizza junkies—I wanted to figure out a way to make my beloved sandwich a little bit healthier to enjoy on a regular basis. Then one summer, when I was staring down a garden full of large zucchini, it came to me: a stuffed zucchini sub! I hollowed out the zucchini, layered it up with all the traditional elements of a meatball sub, then baked it until the whole thing was melty, bubbling perfection.

Whole milk

Bread

Meatballs

2 tablespoons extra-virgin olive oil

1 large egg

¼ cup whole milk

1½ teaspoons kosher salt

¼ teaspoon freshly ground black pepper

½ cup day-old bread torn into ¼-inch pieces

½ pound ground beef (80/20 is ideal, but 85/15 or 90/10 will work)

½ pound lean ground pork

2 tablespoons grated Parmesan cheese

2 tablespoons roughly chopped fresh herbs, such as parsley, basil, or a mix

3 garlic cloves, minced

To Assemble

3 large zucchinis, halved lengthwise

2 tablespoons extra-virgin olive oil

Kosher salt

2 cups prepared or store-bought marinara sauce, warmed

½ cup shredded melting cheese, such as mozzarella, Monterey Jack, fontina, or Swiss

Torn fresh basil leaves, for serving (optional)

- **Make the meatballs:** Place an oven rack 6 to 7 inches from the broiler. Preheat the oven to 400°F.

- Use your hands or a pastry brush to evenly spread the oil over a baking sheet. Set aside.

- In a large bowl, whisk together the egg, milk, salt, and pepper. Add the bread and let it sit for about 5 minutes to absorb the liquid. Add the ground beef, ground pork, Parmesan, herbs, and garlic and use your hands or a rubber spatula to mix until just combined. Form the mixture into 1-inch balls and arrange them on the prepared pan.

- Turn the meatballs in the oil so they are coated on all sides. Bake for 15 minutes, or until the meatballs are browned and cooked through. Remove the meatballs but keep the oven on.

- **Assemble:** Use a teaspoon to scoop out the seeds from the center of the zucchini, creating a well. Rub the oil all over the zucchini halves and season with the salt. Place the zucchini cut side down on a baking sheet and roast for 20 minutes, or until the zucchini is browning on the bottom and is tender but still holding its shape. Set aside to cool.

- Increase the oven temperature to a low broil.

- Flip the zucchini halves so they're cut side up on the baking sheet. Fill each half with enough sauce to coat the scooped portion. Top with 4 or 5 meatballs, depending on how large your zucchinis are, followed by more sauce to coat the meatballs. Sprinkle the cheese evenly over the top and broil for 5 minutes, or until the cheese is melted and golden brown. Sprinkle with basil, if desired, and serve with any remaining sauce.

Note

A great time-saver is doubling the meatball recipe and holding the leftovers for dinner another night. Keep them in an airtight container in the refrigerator for up to 4 days, or in the freezer for up to 3 months. (The meatballs also happen to be a great way to use up older bread!)

Parmesan Rind Cacio e Pepe

Parmesan rinds are such a gold mine of flavor that I had to include two recipes that put them to good use (the other being Parmesan Cream Scalloped Potatoes on page 152). This dish is the perfect example of how tossing in the rinds to let their flavor infuse is a major level-up for a small handful of kitchen staples (butter, garlic, pasta), turning them into a complete and crave-worthy dish.

2 or 3 (3- to 4-inch) Parmesan cheese rinds

1 (16-ounce) box spaghetti

6 tablespoons unsalted butter

4 garlic cloves, sliced

1 teaspoon kosher salt, plus more for pasta water

1 teaspoon freshly ground black pepper, plus more to taste

- Using a Microplane or cheese grater, grate off any remaining bits of Parm from the rind. Set aside.

- Fill a large pot with cold water (as much as you'd use to make pasta). Add the Parmesan rinds, salt generously, and, over high heat, bring the water to a boil. Add the spaghetti and cook for a few minutes less than the package directions so the pasta is slightly more undercooked than al dente. Strain the pasta but reserve all the cooking water as well as the Parmesan rinds. Set aside.

- Melt the butter in a large sauté pan over medium heat. Add the garlic and salt and cook until the garlic is golden and fragrant, about 2 minutes. Add 1 cup of the reserved pasta water along with the rinds. Increase the heat to medium-high to bring the sauce to a rapid simmer. Cook until the sauce is reduced slightly and infused with Parmesan flavor, about 4 minutes. Remove the rinds and discard.

- Keeping the pan over medium-high heat, add the pasta to the sauce with the black pepper and toss to evenly coat. Add 1 cup of the cooking water and bring to a simmer. Cook, stirring constantly, until the pasta is cooked to al dente and the sauce clings to the pasta, 3 to 4 minutes. If the sauce thickens too much before the pasta is done cooking, add additional cooking water (up to 2 cups).

- Divide the pasta among four serving bowls and top with the reserved grated Parmesan and black pepper to taste.

The Dairy Dregs

I think we can all agree that there is nothing more frustrating than the knob of cream cheese that wouldn't cover a bagel, the few tablespoons of yogurt that wouldn't qualify as breakfast, and the scant cup of buttermilk that is barely pancake-capable. And while we're all having this very real moment together, let's also agree that what usually happens is these items sit in our refrigerator—even though we have the best of intentions to use them—only to get pitched during the next clean-out. But our dairy deserves better than that! These ingredients, even in small amounts, can be just the thing for bringing a dish together and fortifying it with rich, creamy goodness. Whether they're being folded into eggs, swirled into sauces, drizzled into desserts, blended into smoothies, or even shaken into cocktails, there's always a way to let these leftovers have their moment.

Cotton Candy Smoothies

I don't think there's anything a smoothie can't do—it's sweet, creamy, filling, and the perfect delivery system for veggies, whether you're trying to get more into the kids or yourself. What I love about this recipe is that it's a blank canvas for tossing in your favorite fruit, especially varieties that turn the smoothie fun cotton candy colors. And there's no better reminder to make this recipe than seeing the last cup of milk in the carton.

Frozen cauliflower

Bananas

1 cup milk of any kind

½ medium banana

1 cup frozen raspberries, blueberries, or mango

½ cup frozen cauliflower

3 tablespoons honey

- In a blender, combine the milk, banana, fruit, cauliflower, and honey and blend until smooth. Enjoy immediately.

Retro Ambrosia Salad

Growing up, whenever there would be extended family dinners or potlucks with friends and neighbors, there was always a big bowl of ambrosia salad on the table. I wanted to give this beloved throwback dish a modern spin by calling for fresh fruit instead of canned and coconut cream whipped topping and Greek yogurt instead of sour cream and traditional whipped topping—which also happens to be the perfect way to use up the remnants of those containers. That said, you could certainly use sour cream, whipped topping, or any other yogurt that you might have.

Pineapple

Cherries

Mini marshmallows

Shredded sweetened coconut

Unsalted pistachios

1 cup whipped topping, defrosted in the fridge (I love using a coconut cream version, but any kind will work)

¼ cup plain whole-milk Greek yogurt

1 cup clementine segments (from about 3 oranges)

1 cup pineapple cut into ½-inch pieces

1 cup cherries, pitted

1 cup mini multicolor marshmallows

½ cup shredded sweetened coconut, toasted in a dry pan

¼ cup unsalted pistachios, toasted in a dry pan

- In a large bowl, stir together the whipped topping and yogurt. Fold in the oranges, pineapple, cherries, marshmallows, coconut, and pistachios. Transfer to a serving bowl and refrigerate for at least 2 hours or up to 1 day before serving.

Smoked Salmon Omelet for One

When it comes to no-brainer breakfasts, nothing beats eggs. While a great omelet doesn't usually need much more than good butter, salt, and pepper (a trick I learned from my friend and chef Ludo Lefebvre), a little extra cream never hurt anybody. In this case, it's a small pat of cream cheese that would otherwise be too skimpy for a bagel. It gives the eggs an even richer, creamier consistency, and it's a natural pairing with smoked salmon. But the most luxurious part? It makes a gorgeous omelet for one. Enjoy with a glass of prosecco and a nice, quiet house. (Or scale up the recipe and share with others.)

Smoked salmon

Fresh chives

3 large eggs

¼ teaspoon kosher salt

1 tablespoon unsalted butter

2 slices smoked salmon (about 1 ounce)

2 tablespoons plain cream cheese, plus more for serving

Minced fresh chives, for serving

- In a medium bowl, whisk together the eggs and salt with 1 tablespoon water.
- Heat a 7- or 8-inch nonstick sauté pan over medium-low heat. Add the butter and cook until it just begins to bubble. Pour in the eggs and, using a rubber spatula, quickly stir them in a figure-eight formation. Continue stirring in this motion until the eggs begin to set, 2 to 3 minutes. Use your spatula to gently lift one edge of the omelet to make sure it's holding together. When ready, remove the pan from the heat and let it sit for an additional minute so the omelet can release from the pan.
- Lay a slice of the smoked salmon down the center of the eggs. Add the cream cheese in small dollops over the salmon. Fold a third of the omelet up and over the filling. Use your spatula to turn the folded portion of the omelet over the last third, so the "seam" is now on the bottom. Tilt the pan toward your serving plate and use your spatula to slide the omelet out of the pan and onto the plate. Top the omelet with the remaining smoked salmon and cream cheese, and sprinkle with the chives. Serve immediately.

Note

You can use any type of cream cheese for this dish—flavored, whipped, nondairy. And this dish can easily be doubled, tripled, or quadrupled—the more cream cheese you have, the more omelets you can make! Alternatively, this would be just as good with goat cheese or ricotta.

OFF
BROIL

Dress-It-Up Dressings

Whenever there's a scant amount of mayo left in the container, that's when I know it's homemade dressing time. These variations on a simple, creamy dressing are leaps and bounds better than anything you could find at the store and are good for so much more than just tossing with salads (although they make that more fun too).

TANGY RANCH DRESSING

This is the perfect all-around dressing, whether you're spreading it on sandwiches; drizzling it over salads and baked potatoes; or using it to dunk roasted vegetables, chicken nuggets, or your pizza (I said it—it's Brady's condiment of choice!).

⅓ cup sour cream

¼ cup mayonnaise

1 tablespoon fresh lemon juice (about ½ lemon)

1 teaspoon Worcestershire sauce

1 garlic clove, minced

¼ teaspoon kosher salt, plus more to taste

¼ teaspoon celery seed

¼ teaspoon freshly ground black pepper, plus more to taste

2 tablespoons minced fresh chives

● In a medium bowl, whisk together the sour cream, mayonnaise, lemon juice, Worcestershire sauce, garlic, salt, celery seed, and black pepper. Season with more salt and/or pepper to taste. Fold in the chives and store in an airtight container for up to 1 week.

JALAPEÑO, CILANTRO, & LIME DRESSING

This dressing is especially tasty with Southwest- or Mexican-inspired salads. It's also fantastic over nachos, quesadillas, or enchiladas, or as a dipping sauce for roasted chicken.

¼ cup mayonnaise

¼ cup fresh cilantro leaves and stems, roughly chopped

½ small avocado, peeled and pitted

½ medium jalapeño, seeded for less heat and roughly chopped (about 1½ tablespoons)

1 scallion (white and green parts), roughly chopped (2 to 3 tablespoons)

1 teaspoon fresh lime juice

½ teaspoon kosher salt, plus more to taste

Freshly ground black pepper

● In a blender, combine the mayonnaise, cilantro, avocado, jalapeño, scallion, lime juice, salt, and pepper. Add ¼ cup water and blend until smooth. Season with more salt and/or pepper to taste. Store in an airtight container in the refrigerator for up to 1 week.

THOUSAND ISLAND DRESSING

In addition to being a classic pairing with greens, I love a schmear of this on a hot sandwich—especially a Where's the Beet Patty Melt (page 110)—or as a dip for my Pull-Apart Pigs in a Quilt (page 235).

¼ cup mayonnaise

3 tablespoons ketchup

2 tablespoons finely chopped dill pickles or sweet relish

1 tablespoon finely chopped red onion

1 teaspoon apple cider vinegar

½ teaspoon sweet paprika

¼ teaspoon kosher salt

● In a medium bowl, whisk together the mayonnaise, ketchup, pickles, red onion, apple cider vinegar, paprika, and salt. Store in an airtight container in the refrigerator for up to 1 week.

Thousand Island Dressing
PAGE 169

Tangy Ranch Dressing
PAGE 168
Jalapeño, Cilantro, & Lime Dressing
PAGE 169

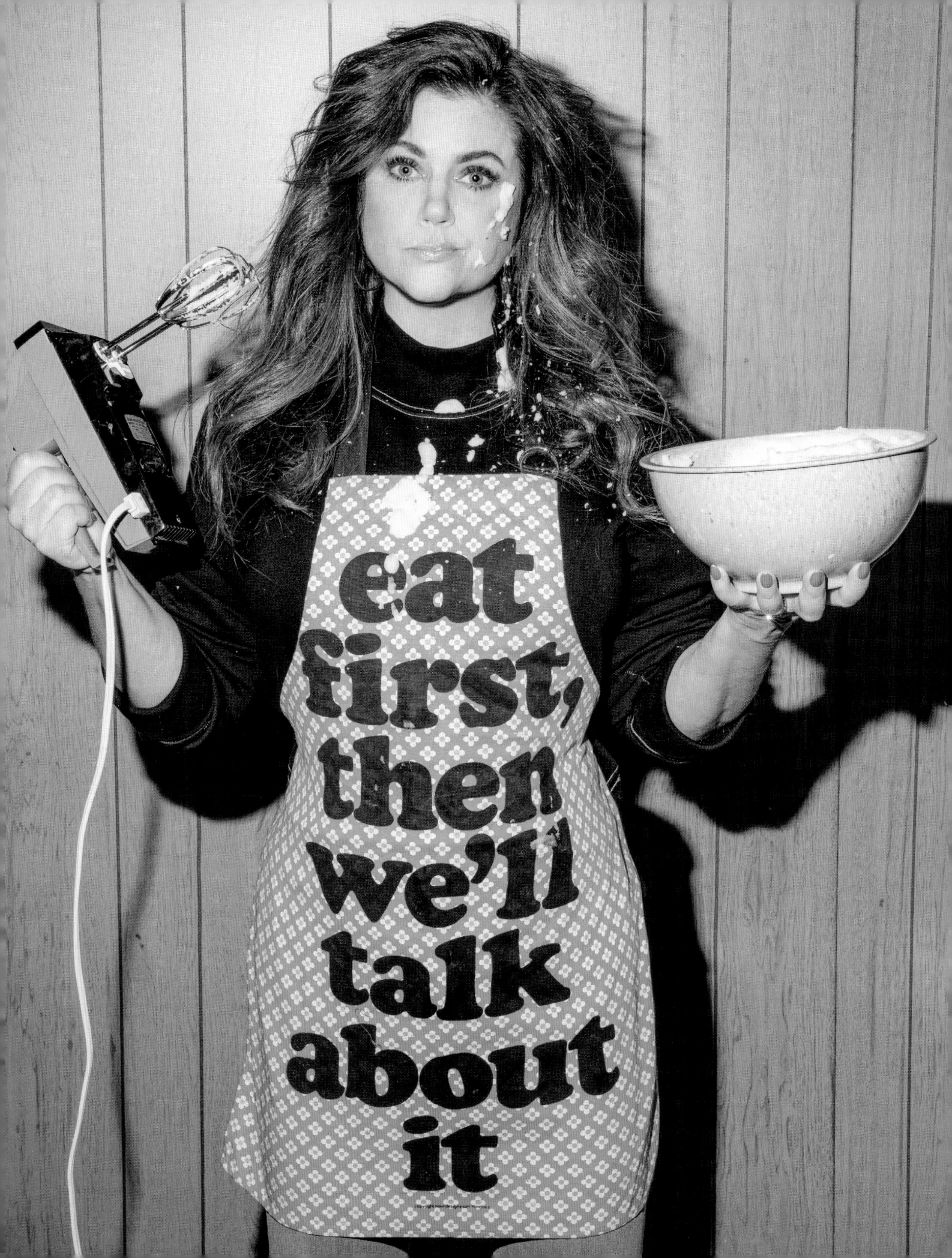
eat
first,
then
we'll
talk
about
it

Buttermilk Horseradish Mashed Potatoes

Finding another use for buttermilk after you've used most of the carton for pancakes or brining chicken can sometimes feel a little bit like being a contestant on *Chopped*, but I assure you that the solution is a simple one: mashed potatoes. While just about any dairy can elevate your puree—milk, cream, cream cheese, mascarpone—I love the tanginess that buttermilk adds. Throw in the subtle zip of horseradish and you have a dish that works as a weeknight side or for the holiday table.

Prepared horseradish

4 large russet potatoes (about 1½ pounds), peeled and cut into 1-inch pieces

1 tablespoon plus ½ teaspoon kosher salt

½ cup buttermilk (or heavy cream, half-and-half, cream cheese, or whole milk)

4 tablespoons unsalted butter, cut into ¼-inch cubes

1 tablespoon prepared horseradish

¼ teaspoon freshly ground black pepper

● In a medium saucepot, combine the potatoes with 1 tablespoon of the salt and cover with 1 inch of cold water. Bring to a boil over medium-high heat. Reduce to a simmer and cook until the potatoes can easily be pierced with a sharp knife, about 10 minutes. Drain the potatoes and return them to the pot. Using a potato masher, hand blender, or stand mixer fitted with the paddle attachment, mash the potatoes until smooth. Fold in the buttermilk, butter, horseradish, the remaining ½ teaspoon salt, and the black pepper. Serve hot or let cool and keep in the refrigerator in an airtight container for up to 4 days.

Chicken alla Vodka

with Anchovy Breadcrumbs

This dish never ceases to amaze me. With just a half cup of cream, an assortment of pantry mainstays (anchovies, breadcrumbs, and tomato paste), and chicken, you can quickly and easily assemble a super-flavorful, downright luxurious dish. I consider it the leftovers silver bullet because I almost always have the ingredients on hand and it's a meal that almost never ends up back in the fridge.

Anchovies

Fresh basil

Panko, plain, or seasoned breadcrumbs

Vodka

Tomato paste

Anchovy Breadcrumbs

2 anchovy fillets

2 tablespoons extra-virgin olive oil

2 tablespoons finely chopped fresh basil

Zest of 1 lemon

½ cup panko, plain, or seasoned breadcrumbs

Chicken alla Vodka

4 boneless, skinless chicken thighs (about 1 pound), cut into 1-inch pieces

1¾ teaspoons kosher salt, plus more to taste

½ teaspoon freshly ground black pepper, plus more to taste

¼ cup extra-virgin olive oil

2 teaspoons dried oregano leaves

1 (16-ounce) box short-cut pasta, such as penne, fusilli, farfalle, or orecchiette

½ small yellow onion, finely diced (about ½ cup)

4 garlic cloves, minced

¾ cup vodka

¾ cup tomato paste

½ cup heavy cream

¼ cup roughly chopped fresh basil leaves

¼ cup grated Parmesan cheese, plus more for serving

1 tablespoon fresh lemon juice (about ½ lemon)

● **Make the breadcrumbs:** In a small sauté pan over medium-low heat, combine the anchovies and olive oil. Cook until the anchovies have melted into the oil, about 1 minute. Add the basil and lemon zest and cook until just fragrant, about 1 minute. Stir in the breadcrumbs and toast, stirring often, until they are golden, 4 to 5 minutes. Transfer the breadcrumbs to a bowl and set aside, or allow them to cool and store in an airtight container in the fridge for up to 2 days.

● **Make the chicken:** Season the chicken thighs with 1 teaspoon of the salt and the pepper.

● Heat the oil in a large sauté pan over medium-high heat. When the oil shimmers, add the chicken in a single layer and sprinkle with the oregano. Stir to coat. Cook until a golden-brown crust forms on the chicken, about 5 minutes. Turn the chicken and cook until the other side is browned and the chicken is cooked through, about 5 more minutes. Transfer to a plate and set aside. Do not wipe out the pan.

CONTINUES

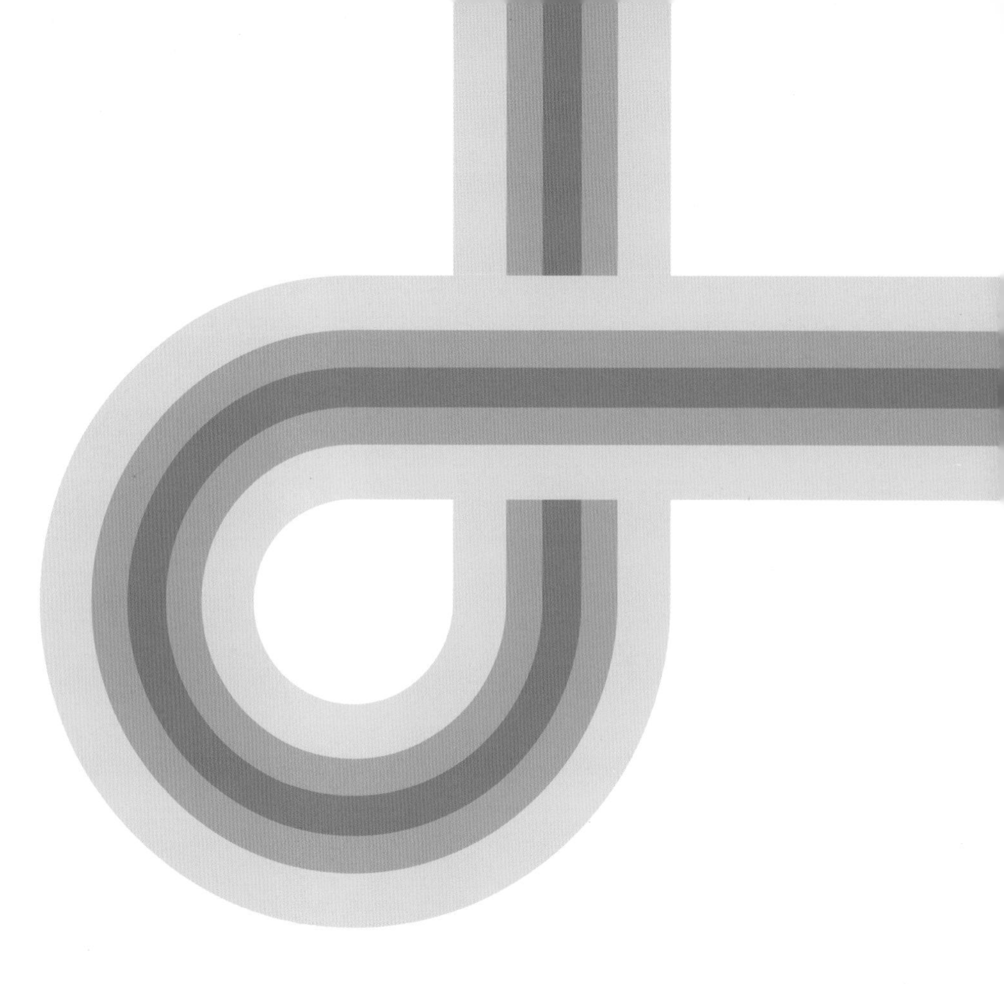

Note

While I love these anchovy breadcrumbs and think they add something really special to the dish, they are completely optional. You'll still have a solidly delicious meal without them. Or, if you want the breadcrumbs and don't want to use the anchovies (or don't have them handy), you can omit them from the breadcrumb recipe. You'll get plenty of fresh pop from the herbs and lemon.

- Bring a large pot of generously salted water to a boil. Add the pasta and cook according to the package directions. Reserve at least 1 cup of the cooking water and drain the pasta. Set aside.

- In the same pan you used for the chicken, combine the onion and garlic over medium heat. Cook until the onions are tender and browned, about 2 minutes. Reduce the heat to low and carefully add the vodka to the center of the pan. Use a wooden spoon to scrape the bottom of the pan to release all the brown bits from cooking the chicken. Quickly whisk in the tomato paste, cream, basil, Parmesan, and the remaining ¾ teaspoon salt. Bring the mixture back to a simmer and cook for 1 to 2 minutes to evenly combine all the ingredients. Taste and add salt and pepper as needed. Add the chicken to the sauce and simmer to warm through, 3 to 4 minutes. Add the cooked pasta and up to 1 cup of the cooking water to create a sauce that clings to the pasta. Finish with the lemon juice and remove the pan from the heat.

- Divide the pasta among four serving bowls and top with more Parmesan and the anchovy breadcrumbs, if using.

The Pink Lady

Leftover egg whites have a ton of uses—egg-white omelets, candied nuts, granola, meringue—but I gotta say that my favorite way to put them to work is in this cocktail. The first time I had a Pink Lady was right after I moved from Long Beach to Los Angeles and I was at a very Hollywood-insider bar, the Formosa. I didn't yet know my Long Island Iced Teas from my Screwdrivers, so I picked this cocktail based on the name and its pretty color. It's been love ever since. The other hack here is to pair any type of fruit liqueur you have with fruit preserves in place of grenadine, which means you'll usually have whatever you need already on hand.

Egg whites

Gin

Handful of ice

3 ounces gin

1 ounce cherry liqueur (or other fruit liqueur)

1 ounce fresh lemon juice (about 1 lemon)

1 ounce syrup from Rescue-Those-Berries Preserves (page 128) or grenadine

1 large egg white

- An hour or two before making your cocktail, place a martini glass in the freezer.
- When ready to serve, fill a cocktail shaker halfway with ice. Add the gin, cherry liqueur, lemon juice, syrup, and egg white. Shake until the cocktail is very chilled and the egg white has become whipped and frothy, about 2 minutes. Strain the cocktail into the chilled martini glass and serve.

Note

If you have multiple egg whites, 1 ounce of egg white is equal to the white of 1 large egg.

The Pink Lady
PAGE 177

Berry-Glazed Sour Cream Doughnuts

I have made peace with the fact that there are some things I could never make in my own kitchen as well as a professional does, like croissants or bagels. But when it comes to doughnuts, as amazing as they can be from some of the bakeries we have here in LA, there's a singular delight to enjoying one hot and fresh out of the oven. I'm especially partial to this recipe, which gets a little lift from just a touch of tangy sour cream (the perfect way to clean out the container!) and a bright fruity kick from a Rescue-Those-Berries Preserves glaze.

Eggs

Sprinkles, freeze-dried fruits, or breakfast cereal

Doughnuts

1 cup all-purpose flour

1 teaspoon ground cinnamon

½ teaspoon baking powder

½ teaspoon baking soda

⅛ teaspoon freshly ground nutmeg

½ cup sour cream or plain Greek yogurt

½ cup packed light brown sugar

¼ cup vegetable oil, plus more for greasing

1 large egg

1 tablespoon pure vanilla paste or extract

Pinch of kosher salt

Glaze

¾ cup sifted confectioners' sugar

¼ cup syrup from Rescue-Those-Berries Preserves (page 128) or other jam/preserve of your choice

Sprinkles, freeze-dried fruits, breakfast cereal, for topping (optional)

- **Make the doughnuts:** Preheat the oven to 350°F. Grease 8 molds in a nonstick doughnut pan with vegetable oil and set aside.

- In a medium bowl, whisk together the flour, cinnamon, baking powder, baking soda, and nutmeg.

- In another medium bowl, whisk together the sour cream, brown sugar, oil, egg, vanilla, and salt. Use a rubber spatula to fold in the flour mixture. Stir until the flour is completely incorporated. Use a piping bag or spoon to divide the batter evenly among the doughnut pan molds, making sure not to fill over the center so your doughnuts come out with a hole.

- Bake for 15 to 18 minutes, until the doughnuts are golden brown and a toothpick or skewer inserted into the center comes out clean. Let the doughnuts cool in the pan until they are easily handled, about 15 minutes, before removing them from the molds and transferring them to a cooling rack to cool completely while you make the glaze.

- **Make the glaze:** In a small bowl, whisk together the confectioners' sugar and preserve syrup until smooth. Depending on the preserves you're using, you may need to add 1 to 2 teaspoons water to thin out the glaze.

- Dip the tops of the doughnuts into the glaze and return them to the cooling rack. Immediately add toppings, if using. Let the glaze set for 5 minutes before serving. These are best enjoyed the day they are made.

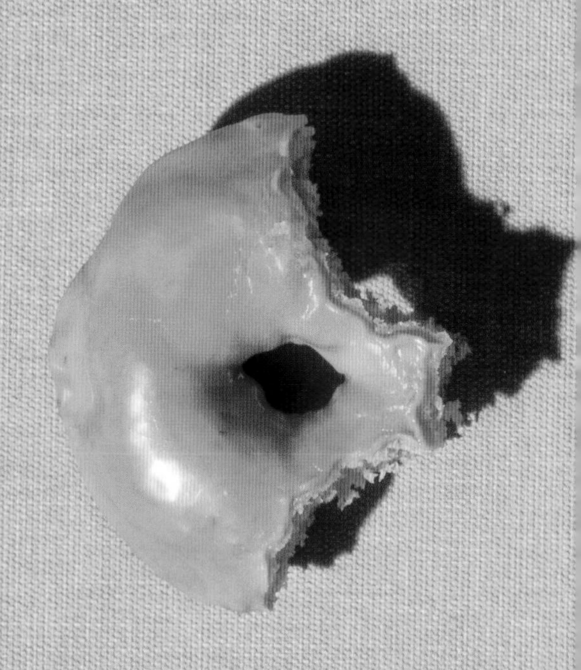

Berry-Glazed
Sour Cream Doughnuts
PAGE 180

Baby Baked Alaskas

And now for the queen of dairy herself: ice cream. Whenever I find myself with several picked-over cartons, I reach for this recipe. You're essentially making ice cream "cupcakes" that get topped with a round of angel food cake or pound cake and crowned with a swirl of meringue. They definitely beat a kiddie-cup-size bowl of ice cream…

Pound cake or angel food cake

Egg whites

Note

You can tailor this recipe to how much ice cream you have available. For small portions, use a cupcake tin. For a good size up from that, try 6- or 8-ounce ramekins, or you can use a pie tin for one large presentation. This meringue recipe makes enough for 4 cupcake-sized servings, but you can double, triple, or even quadruple the ingredients depending on the size of your ice cream stash.

Filling

Nonstick spray

1⅓ cups ice cream (any flavor), softened at room temperature

4 (½-inch-thick) slices pound cake or angel food cake

Meringue

2 large egg whites, at room temperature

¼ cup confectioners' sugar

⅛ teaspoon cream of tartar

- **Make the filling:** If using a standard cupcake tin, spray each cup with nonstick spray and line with a piece of plastic wrap. (The spray is just to help the plastic wrap evenly line the mold. If you're using a silicone cupcake mold, there's no need for plastic wrap.) Scoop the ice cream into the cups so the ice cream comes two-thirds of the way up the sides. Press down on the ice cream with the back of the spoon to make sure the tin is packed full.

- Use a biscuit cutter or an upside-down glass to cut the cake into rounds that will fit into the top third of the muffin cups. Press the cake gently into the ice cream so they adhere together. Wrap the muffin tin with plastic wrap and freeze to set completely, at least 4 hours or up to overnight.

- **When ready to serve, make the meringue:** In the bowl of a stand mixer fitted with the whisk attachment, combine the egg whites, confectioners' sugar, and cream of tartar. Whip on high speed until stiff peaks form, about 3 minutes.

- Remove the cakes from their cups and place them on a baking sheet, cake side down. Cover the sides and tops of the cakes with meringue and use a brûlée torch to toast the meringue. Serve immediately.

Bottom of the Bag, Box, & Bottle

This chapter is my salute to the unsung heroes of my cooking: crumbs, grounds, last drops, and other tasty morsels that don't get very much love once their whole counterparts are gone. In other words, the left-*behinds* more so than the leftovers. When used in just the right way, they can take a dish to the next level in flavor and texture—whether it's turning my kids' favorite snacks into a dredge for fried chicken or a goat cheese appetizer, reviving slightly stale chips by simmering them in sauce and drizzling them with fresh crema, or transforming the final sips of a wine or spirit bottle into a crowd-pleasing spritzer or a grown-up granita. (Because I wouldn't dream of wasting a single drop!)

These recipes are also the perfect reminder that cooking doesn't always have to feel so inside-the-lines. Pulling together a home-cooked meal can be fun and creative, and that begins with what you see as ingredients when you look around the kitchen. By keeping an open mind about what you can turn into dinner, dessert, appetizers, or cocktails, not only will you be cutting down on your food waste, but you'll also become a more intuitive cook.

Who Left the Chip Bag Open? Chilaquiles

My husband is many wonderful things. But a closer of chip bags? Not one of them. Luckily, we're big fans of Tex-Mex food in my house owing to Brady's proud Texas roots, and stale, slightly chewy tortilla chips happen to be perfect for one of our favorite dishes, chilaquiles. Chilaquiles was actually created as a way to use up older tortillas, which would be fried then simmered in a flavorful sauce. In our case, we're just skipping the frying step and tossing in a big handful of chips. Top it off with scrambled eggs and some crema or sour cream, and you have yourself the perfect breakfast—especially if you've had a few too many the night before.

Cotija cheese

Sour cream or crema

Red onion

Radishes

2 cups store-bought green or red enchilada sauce

4 heaping cups tortilla chips, preferably stale

6 large eggs

½ teaspoon kosher salt

¼ teaspoon freshly ground black pepper

3 tablespoons vegetable oil

½ cup crumbled cotija cheese

½ cup store-bought crema or sour cream

2 medium avocados, peeled, pitted, and sliced

4 small red radishes, thinly sliced (about ⅓ cup)

2 medium jalapeños, thinly sliced

¼ cup finely chopped red onion

Fresh cilantro leaves, for serving

● Add the enchilada sauce to an 8- or 10-inch sauté pan over medium heat. Bring the sauce to a simmer, then lower the heat to medium-low. Add the tortilla chips and toss to coat with the sauce. Cook until the chips begin to soften, about 2 minutes. Remove the pan from the heat and set aside.

● In a small bowl, whisk the eggs with the salt and pepper. Heat the oil in a small nonstick pan over medium heat. Swirl the pan to evenly coat the bottom of the pan with the oil. Add the eggs and use a rubber spatula to stir as they cook, about 4 minutes. Remove the pan from the heat and set aside.

● Transfer the chilaquiles to a serving plate. Top with the cotija and a drizzle of crema, followed by the scrambled eggs, avocado, radish, jalapeño, red onion, and cilantro. Serve hot.

Who Left the Chip Bag Open? Chilaquiles
PAGE 188

Bottom of the Pot Mocha Iced Latte

This is a true glass-half-full moment—that last ½ cup of coffee in the pot is really just an opportunity to make this delicious, refreshing iced latte. My trick for an even more flavorful drink that doesn't get watered down is to make "mocha" ice cubes with cocoa powder and nut or oat milk (or any kind of milk that you have in the fridge), which I keep stashed in the freezer anytime I want an artisanal coffeehouse-caliber drink.

Milk of any kind

Mocha Ice Cubes

1 cup nondairy milk or milk of choice

1½ tablespoons unsweetened cocoa powder

1 tablespoon cane sugar (optional)

To Assemble

1 cup nondairy milk or milk of choice

½ cup brewed coffee, at room temperature or chilled

Unsweetened cocoa powder, for serving (optional)

- **Make the mocha ice cubes:** In a small saucepan over medium heat, combine the milk, cocoa powder, and sugar, if using. Bring to a simmer, stirring to dissolve the cocoa and sugar into the milk, about 2 minutes. Remove the pan from the heat and let the mixture cool before pouring it into ice cube trays and freezing overnight. Remove the ice cubes from the tray and use immediately, or store them in a zip-top bag in the freezer for up to 6 months.

- **Assemble:** Using a milk frother, a whisk, or a mason jar, whip, whisk, or shake the milk until frothy. Place 3 or 4 mocha ice cubes in a glass and top with the coffee, followed by the frothed milk. Dust with cocoa powder, if using. Enjoy.

Note

If the nondairy milk you're using is already sweetened, add the recipe's sweetener as needed. You can also make the mocha ice cubes without any sweetening and the drink will still be delightful.

Pretzel-Crumb Cheese Ball

I love entertaining in the evening, and not necessarily for dinner. Between game nights, movie nights, and cocktail parties, I'll take any excuse to eat a whole bunch of appetizers, keep everyone's glass full, and have a great time. When it comes to the food, I like focusing the menu on bite-sized nibbles and dips, and everything's got to hit the spot in all the right salty, creamy, crunchy ways. This appetizer checks every box and gets big points in the flavor and texture departments, thanks to those valuable crumbs at the bottom of the pretzel bag.

Plain cream cheese

Goat cheese

Shredded cheese, such as cheddar, Monterey Jack, or mozzarella

Fresh chives

¾ cup cream cheese, at room temperature

½ cup goat cheese, at room temperature

¼ cup grated Parmesan cheese

2 teaspoons fresh lemon juice

1 garlic clove, minced

½ teaspoon kosher salt

¼ teaspoon freshly ground black pepper

1 cup shredded cheese, such as cheddar, Monterey Jack, or mozzarella

¼ cup minced fresh chives

1 cup crushed pretzels

Fruits, veggies, crackers, or chips, for serving

- In the bowl of a stand mixer fitted with the paddle attachment or in a large bowl with a hand blender, combine the cream cheese, goat cheese, Parmesan, lemon juice, garlic, salt, and pepper. Blend on high speed until the cheeses are evenly incorporated and smooth, 1 to 2 minutes. Add the shredded cheese and chives and mix on high until evenly combined, about another minute.

- Lay out a 10 x 10-inch sheet of plastic wrap on a cutting board and add the cheese mixture to the center. Bring up the sides of the plastic wrap so the cheese is covered and use the plastic wrap to help form the mixture into a ball. Twist the ends of the plastic wrap together to seal. Place the ball in a bowl and refrigerate until firm, at least 3 hours or up to overnight.

- Add the crushed pretzels to a large plate or rimmed baking sheet. Remove the cheese ball from the plastic wrap and roll it in the pretzels, gently pressing the ball into the pretzels to help them adhere until they cover the ball completely. Use your hands to scoop up any loose crumbs and press them into the cheese ball. Serve with any of your favorite fruits, veggies, crackers, or chips.

Pretzel-Crumb Cheese Ball
PAGE 194

Cheese Cracker-Fried Chicken Sandwiches

I think of this recipe as less of a kitchen hack and more of just the best fried chicken sandwich ever. With perfectly crispy, juicy chicken, all the veggie toppings, and a drizzle of Tangy Ranch Dressing (page 168), it's the kind of meal that I sometimes can't believe came out of my kitchen. The added bonus is that instead of using breadcrumbs to dredge the chicken, I'm using up whatever half-eaten bag of cheesy, crunchy things has been sitting in the pantry—Cheez-Its, Goldfish, Cheetos, Doritos, you name it. My chicken gets an extra-flavorful boost, my kids get a kick out of seeing their favorite snack on their dinner plate, and I get one step closer to cleaning out the snack drawer.

Buttermilk

Iceberg lettuce

½ cup buttermilk

1 teaspoon dried basil leaves

1 teaspoon granulated sugar

½ teaspoon paprika

½ teaspoon dry mustard powder

½ teaspoon celery salt

½ teaspoon onion powder

½ teaspoon garlic powder

¼ teaspoon freshly ground black pepper

4 boneless, skinless chicken thighs (about 1 pound)

½ cup all-purpose flour

2 cups crushed cheesy crackers or chips of your choice, such as Cheez-Its, Goldfish, Doritos, or Cheetos

Vegetable oil, for frying

½ cup Tangy Ranch Dressing (page 168), or store-bought ranch dressing

4 brioche burger buns (or your favorite burger buns), toasted, if desired

1 cup shredded iceberg lettuce, for serving

8 tomato slices, for serving

Sliced pickles, for serving

- In a large bowl, whisk together the buttermilk, basil, sugar, paprika, mustard powder, celery salt, onion powder, garlic powder, and pepper. Add the chicken thighs and toss to coat well. Transfer the bowl to the refrigerator so the chicken can marinate for at least 3 hours or up to overnight.

- Add the flour to a shallow dish. In another shallow dish, add the crushed chips. Remove the chicken thighs from the marinade and let any excess drip off. Coat the chicken thighs on both sides with flour and then gently tap to remove any excess. Add the chicken thighs back into the marinade to coat and again allow any extra to drip off. Finally, add the chicken to the crushed crackers and press firmly so the crumbs adhere to both sides. Set aside on a plate.

- Line a baking sheet with paper towels and set aside.

CONTINUES

Note

This recipe is also handy if you have a little bit of buttermilk you need to use up since it only calls for ½ cup. Also, when cooking the chicken, if your chicken is browned but not cooked through, you can transfer it to a 400°F oven and cook until the chicken is cooked completely.

- In a large sauté pan over medium-high heat, add enough oil to come ½ inch up the sides of the pan. Heat until the oil shimmers or registers 325°F on a thermometer. Working in batches if necessary to not overcrowd the pan, add the chicken thighs and cook until the outside is crispy and golden brown and the chicken is cooked through, 3 to 4 minutes per side. The chicken is done when an instant-read thermometer inserted into the thickest part reaches 165°F. Transfer the chicken to the prepared baking sheet.

- Spread the ranch dressing over both halves of each bun. Top each bottom bun with ¼ cup of the lettuce, tomato slices, pickle slices, and the fried chicken. Add the top bun and serve hot.

Nut-Crusted Fish

This recipe is the answer to two cooking conundrums: How do I make great-tasting, perfectly cooked fish at home? And what do I do with the bag of nuts that's been hanging out in my pantry/freezer? Coating fish fillets with a breadcrumb and chopped nut mixture and baking them in the oven is not only the easiest way to make great fish, but also will ensure that you get a perfectly golden crust and moist, flaky fish every single time.

Panko breadcrumbs

Nuts, such as almonds, pistachios, walnuts, or hazelnuts

Fresh dill and parsley

Note

You can use salted or unsalted and roasted or unroasted nuts for this preparation. If using salted nuts, you'll just adjust the amount of salt used in the nut mixture.

¼ cup plus 4 teaspoons extra-virgin olive oil

4 (6- to 8-ounce) center-cut, skinless fish fillets, such as salmon, halibut, sea bass, or cod

1 teaspoon kosher salt, plus more to season the fish

½ teaspoon freshly ground black pepper, plus more to taste

¾ cup panko breadcrumbs

½ cup roughly chopped nuts, such as almonds, pistachios, walnuts, or hazelnuts (see Note)

¼ cup roughly chopped fresh dill

¼ cup roughly chopped fresh parsley leaves

Zest and juice of 1 lemon

- Preheat the oven to 375°F.
- Lightly brush both sides of each fillet with 1 teaspoon of the oil. Sprinkle both sides with salt and pepper and place the fish bottom side down on a rimmed baking sheet.
- In a medium bowl, stir together the breadcrumbs, nuts, dill, parsley, the remaining olive oil, lemon zest, and pepper until just combined. If your nuts are unsalted, add the salt and stir to combine. If the nuts are salted, taste the mixture before seasoning with more salt to taste. Divide the mixture evenly among the fillets and use your hands to pack it onto the top of each piece of fish. Bake for 12 to 15 minutes, until the fish is firm to the touch and the top is golden brown and crispy. Serve immediately with a sprinkle of the lemon juice.

Coffee-Glazed Pork Ribs

When you're married to a man whose love language is BBQ, you learn a thing or two about what makes the best ribs. After years of experimenting, I've finally discovered that the secret to falling-off-the-bone tender meat plus a smoky char is a two-step process. First, the meat is steamed in a flavorful broth with an assist from your cocktail cart (I like using the last pour of bourbon, because what goes better with barbecue?). Then it is shellacked in a sweet, sticky glaze made complex thanks to a couple of tablespoons of ground coffee. And the best part? No smoker required. You can make these bad boys right in the oven.

SERVES 4

Low-sodium chicken, vegetable, or beef stock

Note

The recipe calls for using bourbon as part of the rub, but you could also use stock (any type), beer, or water.

Coffee Glaze

1 cup low-sodium chicken, vegetable, or beef stock

2 tablespoons ground coffee

3 tablespoons ketchup

2 tablespoons molasses (any type)

1 tablespoon vegetable oil

1 tablespoon Worcestershire sauce

1 teaspoon yellow or Dijon mustard

½ teaspoon unsweetened cocoa powder

¼ teaspoon freshly ground black pepper

Ribs

1 slab (about 3 pounds) pork spareribs

½ cup bourbon (see Note)

2 teaspoons kosher salt

1 teaspoon garlic powder

1 teaspoon onion powder

1 teaspoon smoked paprika

1 teaspoon dry mustard powder

½ teaspoon ground cinnamon

½ teaspoon cayenne pepper

¼ teaspoon freshly ground black pepper

- **Make the glaze:** In a small saucepan over medium-high heat, bring the stock to a boil. Remove the pan from the heat and stir in the ground coffee. Let the coffee steep for 6 minutes before straining the liquid into a small bowl. Discard the coffee grounds.

- Return the coffee stock to the pot and add the ketchup, molasses, oil, Worcestershire, mustard, cocoa powder, and pepper. Stir to combine. Over medium heat, bring the mixture to a rapid simmer and cook until the sauce reduces to the consistency of a thick syrup, about 6 minutes. Remove the pot from the heat and let cool (the glaze will thicken slightly as it cools).

- **Make the ribs:** Place an oven rack in the top third of your oven. Preheat the oven to 350°F.

- Place the ribs bone side down on a baking sheet. Pour the bourbon evenly over the ribs.

● In a small bowl, whisk together the salt, garlic powder, onion powder, paprika, mustard powder, cinnamon, cayenne pepper, and black pepper. Spread the spice rub evenly over the ribs. Place the ribs bone side down on the tray and tightly cover the baking sheet with foil. Bake for 1 hour and 30 minutes, or until the meat starts to pull back from the bones and a paring knife easily slips into the thickest part of the meat. Remove the ribs from the oven and increase the temperature to 425°F.

● Use the foil covering as a tray to hold the ribs while you pour off the liquid left in the baking sheet into the coffee glaze. Return the ribs to the baking sheet. Spread the glaze over the top of the ribs and bake for 10 minutes, or until the glaze sets on the ribs and begins to char in places. Let the ribs rest for 10 minutes before slicing and serving with the remaining glaze on the side.

COFFEE

Coffee-Glazed Pork Ribs
PAGE 204

Pickle-Brined Sauerbraten

This recipe was made for those chilly fall and winter months when all you want to eat are cozy dishes cooked low and slow in the oven. Sauerbraten is essentially a German roast, and in addition to braising in an aromatic broth, the meat also is marinated beforehand. Traditionally, sauerbraten takes a luxurious soak in a wine and vinegar mix with lots of garlic and spices, so I found that the perfect cheat is to use the leftover brine from your pickle jar. The result is deeply flavored juicy and tender meat served with a rich pan sauce. It's a great match for my Buttermilk Horseradish Mashed Potatoes (page 173).

Red wine

Fresh thyme and rosemary

3 cups red wine (anything you'd drink)

1 cup pickle juice, white vinegar, or a mix of the two

3 dried or fresh bay leaves

4 garlic cloves, smashed

20 whole allspice berries

20 whole black peppercorns

12 whole cloves

12 juniper berries (crushed cardamom pods or caraway seeds will work too)

4 sprigs fresh thyme, leaves removed from stems

2 sprigs fresh rosemary, leaves removed from stems

2 pounds beef chuck or top round roast

1 teaspoon kosher salt, plus more to taste

Freshly ground black pepper, to taste

¼ cup vegetable oil

3 medium carrots, roughly chopped (about 2 cups)

1 medium fennel bulb, cored and chopped (about 2 cups)

1 large yellow onion, chopped (about 2 cups)

4 tablespoons unsalted butter

2 tablespoons all-purpose flour

⅔ cup raisins, soaked in warm water for 15 minutes and drained

Chopped fresh parsley, for serving

Buttermilk-Horseradish Mashed Potatoes (page 173), for serving (optional)

- In a large bowl, combine the wine, pickle juice, bay leaves, garlic, allspice berries, peppercorns, cloves, juniper berries, thyme, and rosemary. Add the beef to the marinade and submerge it completely. Transfer the bowl to the refrigerator and let the beef marinate at least overnight or up to 5 days. The longer the meat marinates, the more flavor it will have. If the meat isn't completely submerged in the liquid, turn the beef a few times a day so it evenly marinates.

- Lower the top rack of your oven enough to make room for a large, lidded pot. Preheat the oven to 375°F.

- Remove the beef from the marinade and pat it dry with paper towels. Reserve the marinade. Generously season the meat with salt and pepper.

CONTINUES

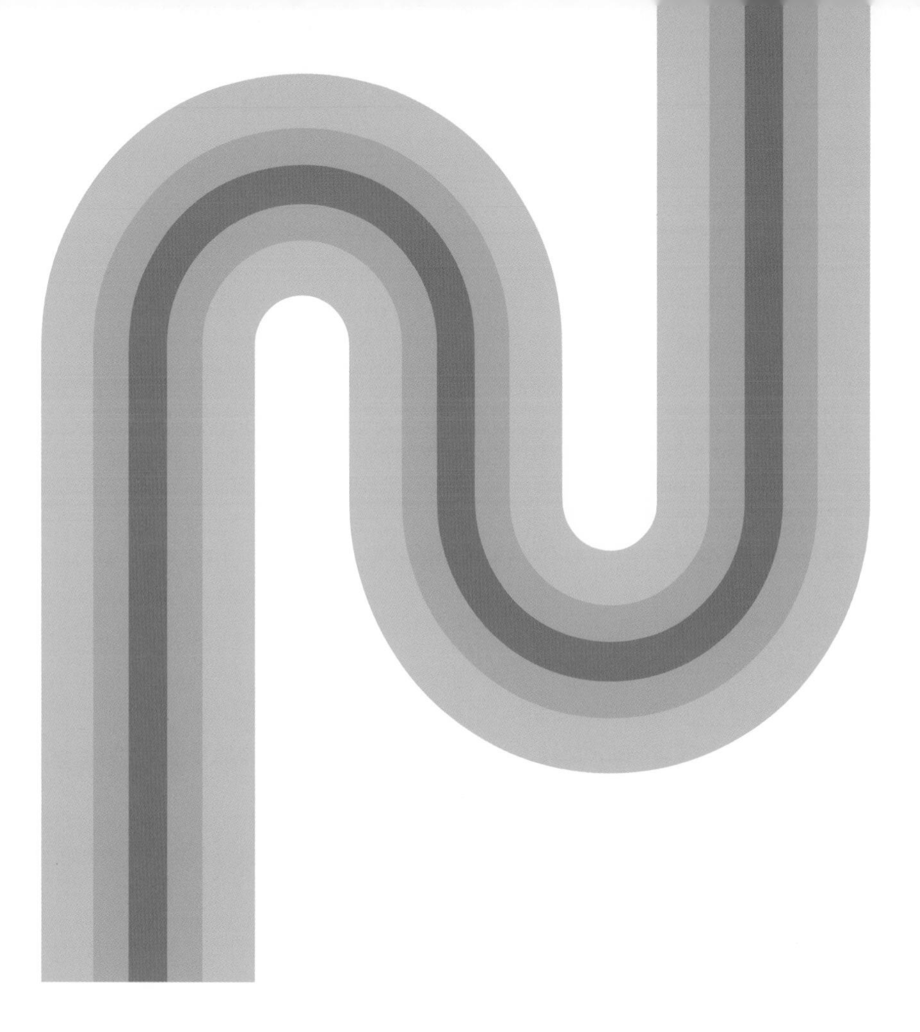

- Heat the oil in a large Dutch oven or large pot with a tight-fitting lid over medium-high heat. Add the meat and sear it on all sides until deeply caramelized, about 8 minutes total. Transfer the meat to a large plate.

- In the same pot over medium-high heat, combine the carrots, fennel, and onion. Cook, stirring and scraping the bottom of the pan often, until the vegetables are tender and browned, 8 to 10 minutes. Add the marinade, scraping the bottom of the pan with a wooden spoon to release any brown bits. Add the meat back in, along with any juices from the plate. Cover with the lid and transfer the pot to the oven. Roast for 1 hour and 30 minutes, or until the meat is fork-tender and sliceable, but not yet falling apart. Transfer the meat to a plate and let it rest while you make the pan sauce.

- Strain the cooking liquid through a fine-mesh sieve into a large bowl and discard the solids. In the same pot over medium-low heat, melt the butter. Sprinkle in the flour and stir until evenly combined. Cook until the roux is a pale golden color, about 3 minutes. Whisk in the strained marinade, add the raisins and 1 teaspoon of salt, and stir to combine. Bring the mixture to a simmer over medium-high heat and cook until the sauce has reduced and coats the back of a spoon, about 10 minutes. Remove the pot from the heat and season with more salt and pepper to taste.

- Slice the meat into ½-inch-thick slices, drizzle with the sauce, and finish with the parsley. Serve with mashed potatoes, if desired.

Cereal Milk Ice Pops

When there's barely enough cereal left for another bowlful, I think the only sensible thing to do is to infuse it into milk, whip it with yogurt, and freeze it into sweet, creamy, cereal-dotted pops. Based on my kids' and their friends' reactions anytime I've made these, they're in complete agreement. I'm partial to the bright colors of Harper's favorite Froot Loops, but any cereal you have would be delicious.

Whole milk

Plain or vanilla whole-milk yogurt

¾ cup whole milk

⅓ cup cane sugar

1 cup cereal of your choice

1 cup plain or vanilla whole-milk yogurt

- In a small saucepan over medium heat, combine the milk and sugar. Bring the mixture to a simmer, stirring often to dissolve the sugar completely. Remove the pan from the heat.

- Add ½ cup of the cereal to a medium bowl. Pour the hot milk mixture over the cereal and steep until the milk cools and the cereal flavors the milk, about 10 minutes. Stir in the yogurt, then fold in the remaining ½ cup of cereal.

- Divide the cereal mixture among 6 ice pop molds. Gently tap the bottom of the molds on a flat surface to ensure that there aren't any air pockets. Add ice pop sticks and freeze overnight.

- If you have any issues removing the ice pops from their molds, dip the molds into a glass of warm water to loosen the ice pops just enough to slide them out of the molds. Serve immediately, or place the ice pops on a parchment-lined baking sheet and freeze them again until firm, about 1 hour, before storing in a zip-top bag for up to 2 months.

Garbage Pound Cake

One of the easiest ways to convince your kiddos to help in the kitchen is to introduce them to the magic of baking. A few ingredients go into a bowl, you pop a dish in the oven, and minutes later you're rewarded with all the sweets you can eat. I get the attraction. The other surefire way to keep them interested is to let them get creative. This recipe combines the best of both worlds. At the foundation is a simple yet rich and buttery cake, which you can then adorn with all manner of odds and ends, such as dried fruit, baking chips, nuts, or coconut flakes. You get to clean out the remnants of your baking drawer, and your kids get to feel the pride of creating their own yummy homemade treat.

Sour cream

Heavy cream

Pound Cake

2 sticks (1 cup) unsalted butter, cut into 1-inch pieces, at room temperature

1½ cups granulated sugar

½ teaspoon kosher salt

½ teaspoon baking powder

5 large eggs, at room temperature

1½ cups all-purpose flour

½ cup sour cream, at room temperature

1 tablespoon vanilla extract or paste

1 cup baking chips, dried fruit, toasted shredded coconut, and/or toasted chopped nuts

Chocolate Drizzle

¼ cup heavy cream

4 ounces chocolate chips or roughly chopped chocolate of any type (½ cup)

- **Make the cake:** Preheat the oven to 350°F. Use 1 tablespoon of the butter to generously grease a 9 x 5-inch nonstick baking dish. If you're using a glass loaf pan and not nonstick, you'll want to line it with parchment paper and leave a 3- to 4-inch overhang on the sides. Glass pans take longer to heat up, which may lead to a longer bake time, so test the cake after the bake time, then continue to bake in 5-minute increments until a toothpick inserted into the center comes out clean. The parchment "handles" will help ensure that it comes out easily.

- In the bowl of a stand mixer fitted with the paddle attachment, combine the remaining butter, sugar, salt, and baking powder. Beat on high speed, scraping down the sides of the bowl every few minutes, until the butter is light in color and very fluffy, about 8 minutes. Lower the speed to medium and add the eggs one at a time, beating well after each addition. Turn the mixer off and scrape down the sides of the bowl. Add ¾ cup of the flour and beat on low to just combine. Add the sour cream and vanilla and increase the speed to medium to mix well. Pause to scrape the sides once again. Add the remaining ¾ cup flour and mix on low until just combined. Use a spatula or wooden spoon to fold in your mix-ins of choice.

CONTINUES

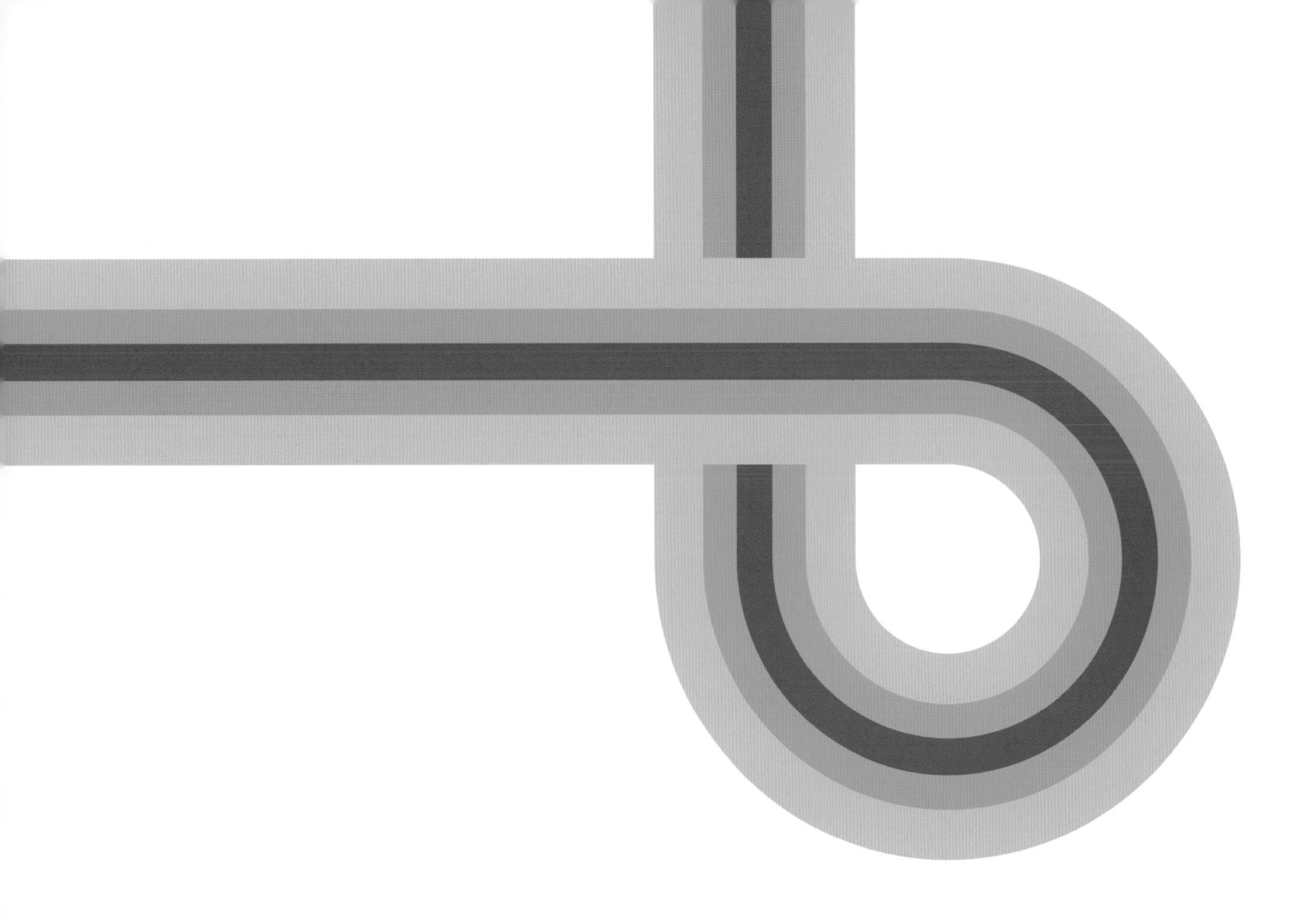

Note

Some of my favorite add-ins to this recipe include raisins or cranberries; chopped dates, apricots, or figs; shredded or flaked coconut; chocolate, butterscotch, or peanut butter baking chips; or pistachios, macadamia nuts, walnuts, and almonds. Also, this recipe includes a chocolate drizzle (because why not), but the cake would be delicious without it as well.

- Add the batter to the prepared pan, making sure to spread the mixture evenly from edge to edge with a rubber spatula to ensure there are no air pockets in the batter. Bake for 1 hour and 15 minutes, or until the loaf is deeply golden brown around the edges, the top just begins to crack, and a paring knife or skewer inserted into the center comes out clean. Let the cake cool in the pan for about 10 minutes before removing the loaf and transferring it to a cooling rack to cool completely.

- **Make the drizzle:** In the microwave or a small pan over medium-low heat, heat the heavy cream until it just begins to steam, 30 seconds in the microwave or about 1 minute on the stove over medium-high heat.

- Add the chocolate to a small bowl and pour the hot cream over the top. Let the mixture sit until the chocolate melts, 2 to 3 minutes, then whisk together. Place the pound cake on a serving plate and drizzle the chocolate over the top. Slice and serve. To store, tightly cover the cake with plastic wrap and store at room temperature for 2 to 3 days.

The Last Pour

You could polish off that barely there pour of wine and move on to the next bottle, *or* you could make a warm-weather spritzer with a smartly paired liqueur, a splash of club soda, and frozen-fruit-as-ice-cubes. I'll admit, I don't wait to make this until I have wine leftovers; it's one of my favorite refreshing cocktails on a hot day.

Handful of assorted frozen fruit, such as berries, sliced peaches, and diced mango (see Note)

4 ounces wine of your choice

4 ounces club soda

2 ounces liqueur (see Note)

- Add the frozen fruit to a highball glass. Top with the wine, club soda, and liqueur. Stir to combine and sip.

Note

For white wines and rosé, I like to go with liqueurs that have floral or herbal notes, such as St. Germain, Strega, Fernet, Cointreau, and Aperol. For reds, I go with Crème de Cassis or Chambord, which have berry-forward flavors. If you don't have frozen fruit, you can use fresh fruit instead and throw in a handful of ice cubes.

IMPORTED BY
VERITAS IMPORTS
GLENDALE, CA
750ML

The Last Pour
PAGE 217

Hurricane Granitas

Whenever I'm having company and I'm not sure whether the last few servings of spirits in a bottle will be enough to stretch, that's when I reach for a batch cocktail recipe. It helps ensure that there's more for everyone, and it's also an opportunity to play with flavor—or in this case, temperature! Here I've taken the flavors of a Hurricane, a classic New Orleans cocktail, and turned them into a boozy frozen treat that works for cocktail hour or dessert.

½ cup cane sugar

¾ cup passion fruit juice

¾ cup fresh or store-bought pulp-free orange juice

½ cup light and/or dark rum

2 tablespoons fresh lime juice

Grenadine, for serving

Note

If you keep the same ratios in place, you can sub in other alcohols and juices to change up the flavors. You can also omit the alcohol completely!

- In a small saucepan over medium heat, combine the sugar with ½ cup water. Bring the mixture to a simmer and stir until the sugar has just dissolved, 3 to 4 minutes. Remove the pan from the heat and set aside to cool completely.

- In a medium bowl, whisk together the cooled simple syrup, passion fruit juice, orange juice, rum, and lime juice. Pour the mixture into an 8 x 8-inch baking dish and freeze for 1 hour. Scrape the granita with a fork to break up any of the forming ice into smaller pieces and return the dish to the freezer. Repeat every 30 minutes until the entire mixture is frozen, about 4 hours total. Let the mixture freeze untouched overnight. Scoop the granita into four serving dishes and top with grenadine to serve.

Squeaky Clean Martinis

When I say "squeaky clean," I'm referring to that bottle of olives you just successfully emptied. As for the martinis, well, those are completely dirty—just the way I like 'em—with plenty of olive brine. There's no better time to make these than after throwing together a batch of Marinated Stuffed Olives (page 136).

Handful of ice cubes

3 ounces gin or vodka

1 ounce dry vermouth

½ ounce green olive juice

Green olives, for serving (optional)

- Chill a martini glass in the freezer for 10 to 15 minutes.
- In a cocktail shaker, combine the ice, gin, vermouth, and olive juice. Shake for at least 1 minute to ensure the cocktail is ice-cold. Strain into the chilled martini glass and serve with olives, if desired.

GIRL, YOU NEED TO
CALM THE F DOWN

Holidays

From the time I was a little girl, the holidays pretty much meant one thing in my family: food. I'd watch as my mom, my grandma, and my aunt would buzz around the kitchen, assembling all the classic dishes, and bring out platter after platter to the table. Between Fourth of July, Thanksgiving, Christmas, Easter, and every birthday and special milestone in between, I got a master class in how to send everyone home very, very full—a tradition I continue to take great pride in. And with all that food comes, of course, the leftovers. Now, I don't have anything against the usual reheat-and-eat, but special-occasion food takes so much time, effort, and love that I think it's destined for more than the microwave. You'll get much more mileage out of the leftovers if you have a plan for giving them another spin, not to mention more opportunities to enjoy them in a fun, new way. That's why I wanted to devote a chapter to reinventing the year's biggest meals, down to the last drop of champagne and the last cube of cheese on your cheese board. From Corned Beef Egg Rolls (page 229) and Latke Breakfast Hash with Greens (page 242) to Trick-or-Treat Fudge (page 236) to a Cranberry Sauce Cocktail (page 245), these recipes will help the celebration last just a little bit longer.

Champagne Crepes (Cheers!)

When you're done toasting to the New Year, your valentine, another trip around the sun, or plain old Tuesday (hey, any occasion is an occasion for bubbles in my book!), you can put your leftover champagne or prosecco to work in these sweet, delicate pancakes. Even if it's been a day or two and your bubbly has lost its fizz, it will still do the trick. You can serve these as is fresh out of the pan, or you can fill or top them with an endless combination of things such as sliced fruit, nut butters, Nutella, chopped nuts, or dried fruit. Cheers!

Whole milk

Note

Since most people don't have an official crepe pan lying around at home, this recipe calls for a nonstick pan, which will do just fine. You can use one of any size and adjust how much batter you use accordingly.

3 tablespoons unsalted butter, plus more for greasing

2 large eggs

¾ cup whole milk

½ cup champagne or prosecco

1 teaspoon pure vanilla paste or extract

1 cup all-purpose flour

¼ cup confectioners' sugar, plus more for serving

Sliced strawberries or other fruits, Nutella, jams, nut butters, chopped nuts, and/or dried fruit

Whipped cream, for serving (optional)

● Melt the butter in a nonstick sauté pan over medium heat. Pour the melted butter into a medium bowl. (Don't wipe out the pan; the excess butter will grease the pan when you add the crepe batter.) Add the eggs, milk, champagne, and vanilla and whisk until just combined. Whisk in the flour and sugar until the batter is smooth.

● In the same pan over medium-low heat, add enough batter to just coat the bottom of the pan. This will be about 2 tablespoons for a small pan or about ¼ cup for a large one. Carefully tilt the pan to help the batter spread evenly. Cook until the underside of the batter is set and just beginning to brown in spots, 30 to 60 seconds. Use a rubber spatula to flip the crepe over and cook for an additional 30 to 60 seconds, until just cooked through. Transfer the crepe to a plate. Continue with the remaining batter, adding a small pat of butter to the pan as needed.

● Fill your crepes with desired fillings, if applicable, and then roll the crepes into rounds or fold them into triangles. Dust with confectioners' sugar to serve and top with whipped cream, if desired.

Corned Beef Egg Rolls

If you, like me, love the excuse to make from-scratch corned beef for St. Patrick's Day—or buy it from the store, no judgment here!—then you now have even more reason to do it. These crispy handheld treats are like mini Reubens with an Irish twist.

Mozzarella cheese

Egg roll wrappers

Thousand Island dressing

Eggs

3 tablespoons extra-virgin olive oil

2 cups shredded brussels sprouts or cabbage

1 medium russet potato, peeled and grated (about 1 cup)

1 teaspoon kosher salt

¼ teaspoon freshly ground black pepper

4 egg roll wrappers

2 ounces julienned corned beef (about ½ cup)

½ cup grated mozzarella cheese

2 tablespoons plus 2 teaspoons Thousand Island Dressing (page 169) or store-bought

1 large egg, beaten

Vegetable oil, for frying

- Heat the olive oil in a large nonstick sauté pan over medium heat. When the oil shimmers, add the brussels sprouts and cook, stirring often, until tender, about 2 minutes. Add the potatoes, salt, and pepper. Cook, stirring often to prevent the potatoes from sticking to the pan, until the brussels sprouts just begin to brown and the potato is cooked through, about 3 minutes. Remove the pan from the heat and let cool.

- Arrange the egg roll wrappers on a clean work surface. Divide the brussels sprout and potato mixture evenly among the wrappers, keeping the filling in the center. Divide the corned beef evenly among the wrappers, laying it over the brussels sprout and potato mixture. Top the corned beef with 2 tablespoons of the grated mozzarella and 2 teaspoons of the dressing.

- Brush the edges of one wrapper with the egg. Fold one of the longer ends up and over the filling, then fold the two shorter ends toward the center as if you were closing a burrito. Continue rolling the wrapper until you have an egg roll. Press the edges firmly against each other so the egg seals it completely. Repeat with the remaining wrappers.

- Line a baking sheet with paper towels and set aside.

- Heat a large sauté pan over medium heat. Add 2 to 3 inches of vegetable oil and heat until it begins to shimmer or registers 350°F on a thermometer. Add the egg rolls and fry until golden brown on the first side, about 90 seconds. Flip and brown on the other side, about another 90 seconds. Transfer the egg rolls to the prepared baking sheet to drain and cool slightly. Serve immediately.

Old-School Ham Salad

This ham salad is the ultimate '70s inspo, and a shout-out to my mom's version, which she'd make every year after the Easter or Christmas ham had been retired to the fridge. I wanted to do her classic recipe justice with plenty of good, creamy texture (the secret is the hard-boiled eggs!) but also give it some modern zip with stone-ground mustard and pickled jalapeños. You can put this out with crackers, scoop it over greens, or pile it onto bread.

Mayonnaise

- 2 cups finely chopped cooked ham
- 4 hard-boiled large eggs, grated
- ⅔ cup finely chopped yellow onion (about 1 small onion)
- ½ cup mayonnaise
- ½ cup pickled jalapeños, minced (I love Jed's)
- 2 teaspoons stone-ground mustard
- 2 teaspoons fresh lemon juice
- ½ teaspoon kosher salt
- ½ teaspoon freshly ground black pepper
- ½ teaspoon paprika

● In a large bowl, combine the ham, eggs, onion, mayonnaise, pickled jalapeños, mustard, lemon juice, salt, pepper, and paprika. Fold together until just combined. Serve immediately with your favorite crackers or chips, or as a sandwich. You can store the salad in an airtight container in the refrigerator for up to 3 days.

Pull-Apart Pigs in a Quilt

An earlier version of this recipe is easily the most popular one on my site, with thousands of people posting it on their social media, sharing it with friends, and telling me how much they and their families loved it. I get the appeal—it's a total feel-good, nostalgic dish that I've given an updated makeover with a garlic-parsley butter, as well as a pretty presentation with them all nestled in a double-decker ring. It's the perfect dish to put together after the Fourth of July, Memorial Day, Labor Day, or any other big grill-out occasion when you find yourself with more hot dogs than you know what to do with.

Fresh parsley

4 tablespoons unsalted butter

4 garlic cloves, minced

2 tablespoons roughly chopped fresh parsley

¼ teaspoon kosher salt

All-purpose flour, for dusting

2 (8-ounce) packages crescent rolls

5 hot dogs, each cut into 4 even pieces

Any Dress-It-Up Dressing (pages 168–69), store-bought dressing, ketchup, or mustard, for serving (optional)

- Preheat the oven to 375°F. Line a baking sheet with parchment paper and set aside.
- Melt the butter in a small sauté pan over medium heat. When the butter starts to foam, add the garlic, parsley, and salt and cook for 1 minute while gently swirling the pan. Remove the pan from the heat and set aside.
- Spread out one tube of the crescent rolls on a lightly floured work surface. Separate the dough on the perforated lines to form 4 squares. Stack the squares on top of one another and use a rolling pin to roll the dough into a 10 x 12-inch rectangle. Lightly flour your rolling pin if it starts sticking to the dough.
- Trim the edges of the rectangle so the lines are as straight and even as possible. Working along the 10-inch side of the rectangle, slice the dough into 5 (2-inch-wide) strips. (A ruler comes in handy here.) Then, cut those strips into 4 (3-inch) pieces. You should now have 20 squares of dough.
- Add a piece of hot dog to each square so that the flat edge of the hot dog lines up in the top corner of a piece of dough. Roll the hot dog so it is covered in dough and use a little bit of water to form a seal. Pinch the bottom excess dough up against the hot dog to seal that side. You should have a little bundle of dough at one end and the hot dog peeking out the other side. Set the pig in the blanket on the prepared baking sheet, seal side down, and repeat with the remaining pieces of dough and hot dogs.
- Arrange 12 of the pigs in a blanket in a ring, with the hot dog side facing out. Shingle the remaining 8 hot dogs in the center of the ring, so that they rest on the back edge of the pigs in a blanket on the bottom ring. (The final shape should look like a flower.) Brush all of the dough with the prepared garlic butter and bake for about 40 minutes. The dough should be golden brown and cooked through. Serve immediately with any desired dipping options.

Trick-or-Treat Fudge

Okay, so Halloween candy doesn't exactly *need* to get used up—nor is that ever a problem in my house—but this recipe is a fun project with the kids (plus, it gives their stash a gentle nudge out the door). It's a traditional chocolate fudge base that gets loaded up with any and all of your favorite treats and would make a cute, themed favor for just about any holiday.

Nonstick spray

3½ cups chocolate chips (milk, semisweet, bittersweet, or white)

1 (14-ounce) can sweetened condensed milk

1 tablespoon pure vanilla paste or extract

Pinch of kosher salt

1 cup assorted Halloween candy, broken or cut into 1-inch pieces if needed

- Spray an 8 x 8-inch baking dish with nonstick spray, and then line with plastic wrap or parchment paper, leaving a 2-inch overhang on two sides. (The nonstick spray will help the paper evenly line the dish and stick to the edges.)

- In a large microwave-safe bowl, combine the chocolate chips and sweetened condensed milk. Microwave for 1 minute and stir with a rubber spatula to incorporate. If not all of the chocolate has melted, microwave in additional 20-second increments, stirring after each one.

- Stir in the vanilla and salt. The consistency will thicken to a hot fudge texture. Evenly spread the fudge in the prepared baking dish and use a rubber spatula to smooth the top. Sprinkle the candy over the top and use your hands to gently press the candy into the chocolate. (If the candy isn't pressed into the fudge, it will not adhere, so don't skip this step!) Transfer the dish to the refrigerator to set for at least 3 hours or up to overnight. When ready to serve, use the plastic wrap "handles" to lift the fudge from the baking dish and cut the fudge into bite-sized pieces. The fudge can be stored in the refrigerator in an airtight container for up to 2 weeks.

TARGET
GOBSTOPPER

Trick-or-Treat Fudge
PAGE 236

Thanksgiving Shepherd's Pie

Shepherd's pie is a traditional English dish that's essentially a meat-and-sauce filling that gets smothered with mashed potatoes and baked until bubbly and golden. So it seems almost too obvious that you should be shredding your leftover turkey, tossing it with your green bean casserole (or canned green beans) and gravy, and topping it off with your mashed potatoes and a little Gruyère that you probably have left over from your cheese board or potato gratin.

Fennel or celery

Carrots

Gruyère cheese

- 2 tablespoons unsalted butter
- ⅓ cup finely chopped fennel or celery
- ⅓ cup finely chopped carrots
- ¾ cup frozen pearl onions or ½ cup chopped yellow onion
- 1 garlic clove, minced
- 2½ cups shredded cooked turkey (chicken will work here too)
- 1 cup prepared gravy
- ¼ cup green bean casserole or canned green beans, drained and rinsed
- 1 teaspoon kosher salt
- ½ teaspoon freshly ground black pepper
- ½ teaspoon dried thyme leaves
- ½ teaspoon dried basil leaves
- 3 cups prepared mashed potatoes
- ½ cup grated Gruyère cheese

● Preheat the oven to 350°F.

● Melt the butter in a large sauté pan over medium heat. Add the fennel and carrots and cook until they have softened and are beginning to brown, about 7 minutes. Add the pearl onions and cook until they are translucent and all the liquid in the pan has evaporated, 3 to 4 minutes. Add the garlic and cook until fragrant, about 1 minute. Stir in the turkey, gravy, green beans, salt, pepper, thyme, and basil and cook until heated through, about 5 minutes. Transfer the mixture to a 1½-quart baking dish and spread it in an even layer. Set aside.

● In a large sauté pan over medium-low heat, cook the mashed potatoes until just warmed through and easy to stir, about 6 minutes. Add half of the grated cheese and stir to combine. Remove the pan from the heat.

● Spread the mashed potatoes evenly over the filling in the baking dish and sprinkle the top with the remaining cheese. Place the baking dish on a sheet tray and bake for 30 minutes, or until heated through.

● Switch the oven setting to broil and broil until the potatoes are golden and bubbly, 2 to 3 minutes. Cool slightly before serving.

Latke Breakfast Hash
with Greens

One of my favorite effortless breakfasts for the whole family is a hash. It's got a little bit of everything—meat, potatoes, veggies, and, of course, fried eggs—and I love knowing that I'm sending full bellies out into the world. This version sticks to the same classic formula but subs in any leftover latkes you have from your Hanukkah party. I also call for adding Swiss chard because by the time the holidays roll around, we usually feel like we can use an extra dose of green on our plates.

3 tablespoons extra-virgin olive oil

2 hot Italian turkey sausage links, casings removed

½ large red bell pepper, stemmed, seeded, and cut into ½-inch pieces (about 1 cup)

½ small yellow onion, cut into ½-inch pieces (about 1 cup)

1 bunch Swiss chard, leaves and stems cut into ½-inch pieces (about 2 cups)

½ teaspoon kosher salt, plus more to taste

¼ teaspoon freshly ground black pepper, plus more to taste

4 (2- to 3-inch) latkes, broken into 1-inch pieces

4 large eggs, cooked your favorite way, for serving

Note

If you don't have any latkes on hand, you could use store-bought frozen hash browns instead. You could also replace the Swiss chard with any other sturdy green, such as kale, mustard greens, or mature spinach.

- Heat the oil in a large sauté pan over medium-high heat. Cook the sausage until it is browned all over, 5 to 6 minutes. Stir occasionally and use your spoon to break the sausage into crumbles. Transfer the sausage to a plate, leaving behind any oil.

- To the same pan over medium-high heat, add the bell pepper, onion, and Swiss chard. Cook until the vegetables are tender and any water they release has evaporated, 4 to 5 minutes. Season with the salt and pepper. Add the latke pieces and return the cooked sausage to the pan. Cook until the latkes are heated through and crisping around the edges, 4 to 5 minutes. Season with additional salt and pepper, if needed. Top with eggs and serve.

Cranberry Sauce Cocktail

This fresh, new cocktail recipe turns your Thanksgiving staple into a cozy, whiskey sour–inspired libation. The more leftover cranberry sauce you have, the more you can make, as this recipe can easily be doubled, tripled, or quadrupled. Yes, please.

Handful of ice

3 ounces bourbon

1½ ounces fresh or store-bought pulp-free orange juice

1 tablespoon cranberry sauce

1 teaspoon superfine sugar (optional, depending on the sweetness of the cranberry sauce)

- Fill a cocktail shaker halfway with ice. Add the bourbon, orange juice, cranberry sauce, and sugar, if using. Shake for 1 minute to fully chill the cocktail and combine the ingredients. Strain the cocktail into a rocks glass with a large ice cube and enjoy!

Cheese Board Pinwheels

We all know how clutch a great cheese board can be when you have a crowd coming over for the holidays, and we also know that the more epic you go, the more likely it is that you'll end up with a fridge full of leftovers. Or in my case, things that didn't even make it onto the board because I got too ambitious! The great news is that all those random tidbits, no matter what variety of cheeses, meats, or olives you have, lend themselves perfectly to this salty, cheesy appetizer. These pinwheels take minutes to make thanks to store-bought puff pastry, and nobody would ever guess that they were happy accidents.

6 ounces cheese, any rinds removed, cut into 1-inch pieces (about 1½ cups)

2 ounces charcuterie, cut into small pieces (about ½ cup)

¼ cup pitted olives

All-purpose flour, for dusting

1 (16-ounce) box puff pastry (2 sheets), defrosted in the refrigerator overnight

- Preheat the oven to 375°F. Line two baking sheets with parchment paper and set aside.
- In a food processor, combine the cheese, charcuterie, and olives. Process, scraping down the sides halfway through, until everything is finely ground and no larger than peas. Set aside.
- On a lightly floured work surface, roll out the first piece of puff pastry into a 12 x 14-inch rectangle. Keep the second sheet of puff pastry in the refrigerator until ready to use. Place pastry so the longer side is parallel to the edge of your counter. Sprinkle half of the cheese mixture evenly over the dough, then roll the dough into a tight log. Use a bit of water and your fingers to help seal the edge of the roll.
- Using a serrated knife, slice the roll into ¼-inch-thick rounds. Lay the rounds flat on the prepared baking sheet, leaving at least 1 inch between them. You can use your hands to re-form the pinwheels into rounds if they flattened when you sliced them. Bake the first half of the pinwheels for 22 minutes, or until the pinwheels have puffed, the cheese is melted, and everything is golden brown.
- While the first batch cooks, assemble the second batch. Serve warm or at room temperature.

Note

These freeze really nicely, which means you could save them for your next gathering. Simply assemble the pinwheels and arrange them on the prepared baking sheet, but instead of baking them, freeze them. Once frozen, you can transfer them to a zip-top bag for up to 2 months. Bake them from frozen, adjusting the cook time to make sure they're heated through.

Pot Roast & Potato Pizza

In our house, pizza isn't just a crowd-pleasing meal that comes together quickly. It's also the perfect canvas for reinventing leftovers. Whether it's Monday's barbecued chicken, Tuesday's shrimp scampi, or Wednesday's roasted squash, you can hardly go wrong when you're pairing these items with other tasty ingredients and piling them up on a doughy crust. The same goes for your holiday leftovers. In this case, we're putting your pot roast (or brisket or pulled pork) to work yet again, along with any leftover potatoes, whether they're roasted fingerlings, potato gratin, dolloped mashed potatoes, or my Parmesan Cream Scalloped Potatoes (page 152).

Broccolini

Fresh parsley

Shredded cheese, such as mozzarella, fontina, or Gruyère

Note

I've included my favorite pizza dough recipe here, but you could also use 1 pound of store-bought dough.

Pizza Dough

1 (.25-ounce) packet active dry yeast

2 teaspoons sugar

1 cup all-purpose flour, plus more for dusting

1 cup whole wheat flour

1 teaspoon kosher salt

2 tablespoons extra-virgin olive oil, plus more as needed

To Assemble

½ bunch Broccolini (about 5 stalks)

3 tablespoons extra-virgin olive oil, plus more for drizzling

Kosher salt

All-purpose flour, for dusting

1 cup shredded cheese, such as mozzarella, fontina, or Gruyère

1½ cups prepared cooked potatoes, such as scalloped potatoes, potato gratin, or roasted fingerling potatoes, chopped into 1-inch pieces

1 cup shredded or sliced cooked pot roast, brisket, or pulled pork

2 tablespoons grated pecorino Romano cheese

3 tablespoons fresh parsley leaves, for serving

Red pepper flakes, for serving (optional)

Freshly grated lemon zest, for serving (optional)

Grated pecorino or Parmesan cheese, for serving (optional)

- **Make the dough:** In a small bowl, combine the yeast, sugar, and ¾ cup warm water. Let the mixture sit until it begins to foam, about 10 minutes.
- In a large bowl, combine the flours and salt. Form a well in the center and add the yeast mixture and olive oil. Use a fork to incorporate the wet ingredients into the dry until a dough forms.
- Turn out the dough onto a lightly floured surface and knead the dough until it is smooth and elastic, about 5 minutes.

- Lightly coat a large bowl with olive oil and add the dough, turning once to coat the dough in the oil. Cover the bowl with plastic wrap or a clean kitchen towel and set the bowl in a warm place to rise until the dough has doubled in size, about 1 hour.

- Cut the dough in half. Wrap one half in plastic wrap and store for another use. It will last in the fridge for up to 1 day and in the freezer for up to 4 months.

- **Assemble:** Place a pizza stone or an upside-down baking sheet in the oven. Preheat the oven to 450°F. Line a baking sheet with parchment paper and set aside.

- On the prepared baking sheet, toss the Broccolini with 1 tablespoon of the olive oil and a sprinkle of salt. Roast for 8 minutes, or until the Broccolini is charred but not completely cooked through and tender. Keep the oven on.

- On a lightly floured work surface, roll the pizza dough into a 12- to 13-inch round. If you are baking the pizza on a baking sheet, do not roll the pizza dough wider than the back of the pan. Transfer the dough to a flour-dusted pizza peel or the back of a second baking sheet. Drizzle the remaining 2 tablespoons olive oil over the pizza dough and sprinkle with salt. Evenly scatter the shredded cheese over the pizza dough and bake for 8 minutes, or until the crust is cooked through and begins to turn golden brown.

- Remove the crust from the oven and top it with the potatoes and pot roast. Lay the Broccolini over the top and sprinkle everything with the pecorino Romano and the olive oil. Return the pizza to the oven and bake for 8 more minutes, or until the crust is a deep golden brown, the toppings are heated through, and the cheese is beginning to brown. Finish the pizza with the parsley leaves and red pepper flakes, lemon zest, and pecorino, if using. Serve hot.

SEE PHOTO
PAGE 250

Pot Roast
& Potato Pizza
PAGE 248

Peppermint Hot Chocolate Cookies

It doesn't get more holiday than peppermint and hot cocoa—or having roughly thirty leftover candy canes—so I've combined the two into one chewy, chocolaty cookie. Finished off with a festive white chocolate drizzle and a candy cane crumble, these are perfect for cookie swaps or for sending home with holiday party guests.

Eggs

White chocolate

Semisweet or bittersweet chocolate chips

Note

The chocolate cookie base is good enough on its own if you want to omit the white chocolate drizzle, or if you don't want to wait until you have leftover candy canes.

Cookies

¾ cup all-purpose flour

2 tablespoons unsweetened cocoa powder

½ teaspoon baking powder

¼ teaspoon kosher salt

6 tablespoons unsalted butter, at room temperature

⅓ cup packed light brown sugar

⅓ cup granulated sugar

1 large egg

¼ teaspoon peppermint extract or vanilla extract

½ cup semisweet or bittersweet chocolate chips

White Chocolate Drizzle

4 ounces white chocolate

3 standard-sized peppermint candy canes, crushed (about ½ cup)

- **Make the cookies:** In a medium bowl, whisk together the flour, cocoa powder, baking powder, and salt. Set aside.

- In the bowl of a stand mixer fitted with the paddle attachment, add the butter and sugars. Beat on medium-high speed until light and fluffy, about 2 minutes. Add the egg and extract and mix to combine. Add the flour mixture and once again mix to combine.

- Add the chocolate chips to a small microwave-safe bowl. Microwave in 30-second increments, stirring after each one, until just melted. Pour the melted chocolate into the cookie dough and beat on low speed until just combined. Remove the cookie dough from the mixer and cover with plastic wrap. Refrigerate for at least 30 minutes or up to overnight.

- Preheat the oven to 375°F. Line two baking sheets with parchment paper.

- Use a tablespoon measure to portion out the cookie dough. Use the palm of your hands to roll each scoop of dough into a ball. Arrange the dough on the prepared baking sheets, leaving about 1½ inches between them. Bake for 10 minutes, or until the cookies are just set around the edges but puffed and soft in the middle. Let cool for a few minutes on the sheet tray before transferring them to a cooling rack to cool completely.

- **Make the drizzle:** Add the white chocolate to a small microwave-safe bowl. Microwave in 30-second increments, stirring after each one, until just melted. Drizzle the melted chocolate across the cookies and immediately sprinkle the crushed candy canes over the chocolate before it sets so they adhere. Let the chocolate set for 15 minutes before serving. Store the cookies in an airtight container at room temperature for up to 4 days.

DEF
ABC
TUV
WXY

Acknowledgments

Brady, Harper, Holt, & my whole family–
My clan, who is willing to try pretty much anything I serve them at the dining table. I love feeding your cute faces.

Rachel, Ali, Rebecca, Jen, Santos–
My peeps, for always supporting my many ideas and helping them come to life. You guys inspire me with your widely creative minds. I truly can't think of a better group to work with.

Nicole, Junie, & Keisha–
My glam crew, for highlighting the goods and covering the not-so-goods.

Brandi, Jai, & Molly–
My handlers, who go to battle for me with grace, kindness, and a dose of kick-ass.

Jeana & Morgan–
My book gals, who embraced my vision from the start and gave me the path to print this baby.

Laura–
My designer, for beautifully putting together all the pieces and helping this book feel just as I intended it.

Additional thanks to the many awesome people who helped contribute to this book–
Le Creuset, Tupperware, CorningWare, Pyrex, Erickson Surfaces, Great Jones, Fiesta Tableware Co., Facture Goods, Modern Fabrics, Smith & Lily, Coppermill Kitchen, Terrain, and Susan Edgington of 345glenhaven.

Index

Page numbers of photographs appear in italics.

A

All-the-Cheeses Spread & Fondue, 138, *140–41*
All-the-Veggies Shakshuka, 114–15, *116–17*
Almond(s)
  Mean Bean Burgers with Saffron Yogurt Sauce, 54, *55*, 56
Anchovy(ies)
  Breadcrumbs, 174, *175*, 176
  Clear-Out-the-Fridge Pasta Salad with Charred Tomato Dressing, 48, *49*
Any-Season Savory Tart, 118–19, *119*
Arancini, Ciao, *46*, 47
Aunt Jenny's Sweet Potato Cake Roll, *130*, 131, 133
Avocado(s)
  Chilaquiles, 188, *190–91*
  Mean Bean Burgers with Saffron Yogurt Sauce, 54, *55*, 56

B

Bacon-Dripping Vinaigrette, 6, *7*, 8
Bagel French Onion Soup, *22*, 23
Baked Alaskas, Baby, *184*, 185
Baked French Toast with Jammy Whip, 2, *3*
Balsamic vinegar
  about, 136
  Marinated Stuffed Olives, 136, *137*
Banana(s)
  Cotton Candy Smoothies, *160*, 162
  Eat Your Veg Muffins with Carrot-Oat Crumble, *100*, 101, 103
Basil, fresh
  Chicken alla Vodka with Anchovy Breadcrumbs, 174, *175*, 176
  Ciao, Arancini, *46*, 47
  No-Frills Frittata, 98, *99*
  Pizza for Breakfast Sandwiches, *18*, 19, 21
  Spaghetti Pie, Oh My! *50*, 51
Bean(s), canned
  Buffalo Chicken, Dip, 36, *37*
  Chipotle Pinto, 86, *87*, 88, *89*
  Mean, Burgers with Saffron Yogurt Sauce, 54, *55*, 56
  Sausage, 'n' Greens, 76–77, *78–79*
Beef
  Corned, Egg Rolls, *228*, 229
  Hamburger Junior VP, 80, *81*
  Pickle-Brined Sauerbraten, 208, *209*, 210, *211*
  Pot Roast & Potato Pizza, 248–49, *250–51*
  Saucy Swedish Meatballs, 24–25, *26–27*
  Something-Borrowed Bourguignon, 82–83, *84–85*
  Stuffed Zucchini "Subs," 156–57, *157*
  Surf & Turf Tacos, 92–93, *94–95*
Beet(s)
  Where's the, Patty Melts, 110–11, *112–13*
Berry(ies)
  Cotton Candy Smoothies, *160*, 162
  Glaze, 180, *182–83*
  Rescue-Those-, Preserves, *128*, 128, *129*
Blue Cheese Buttah, 146, *147*, *148–49*
Bottom of the Pot Mocha Iced Latte, *192*, 193
Bourbon
  Bagel French Onion Soup, *22*, 23
  Coffee-Glazed Pork Ribs, 204–5, *206–7*
  Cranberry Sauce Cocktail, *244*, 245
Bread
  Bagel French Onion Soup, *22*, 23
  Baked French Toast with Jammy Whip, 2, *3*
  Cheddar & Sage, Pudding, 12, *13*
  Everything Croutons, 9, *10–11*
  Greek to Me, New to You Pita Salad Bowls, 14–15, *16–17*
  Roasted Squash, Salad, 6, *7*, 8
  Saucy Swedish Meatballs, 24–25, *26–27*
  Stuffed Zucchini "Subs," 156–57, *157*
Breadcrumbs
  Anchovy, 174, *175*, 176
  Ciao, Arancini, *46*, 47
  Lemony Breaded Pork Chops, 28–30, *29*
  Nut-Crusted Fish, *202*, 203
  Tuna Salad Cakes, 70–71, *71*
Bread pudding, Cheddar & Sage, 12, *13*
Broccoli
  Creamy, Soup with Cheddar "Crackers," 122–23, *123*
  Mimi's Chicken & Rice Casserole, *52*, 53
Broccolini
  Pot Roast & Potato Pizza, 248–49, *250–51*
Brussels sprouts
  Corned Beef Egg Rolls, *228*, 229
Buffalo Chicken Bean Dip, 36, *37*
Burgers, Mean Bean, with Saffron Yogurt Sauce, 54, *55*, 56
Burritos, Grilled Pulled Pork, 86, *87*, 88, *89*
Butter
  Blue Cheese Buttah, 146, *147*, *148–49*

Herbed Brown, *150*, 151
Miso, 155
Buttermilk
Cheese Cracker-Fried Chicken Sandwiches, 198, *199*, 200
Chocolate Spud Cake, 64, *65*, 66, *67*
Eat Your Veg Muffins with Carrot-Oat Crumble, *100*, 101, 103
Horseradish Mashed Potatoes, 173
Butternut Squash Quesadillas, 124–25, *126–27*

C

Cabbage
Corned Beef Egg Rolls, *228*, 229
Mashed Potato Dumpling Soup, 42–43, *44–45*
Slaw, 58, *59*, 60
Surf & Turf Tacos, 92–93, *94–95*
Caesar Dressing, 9, *10–11*
Cake
Aunt Jenny's Sweet Potato, Roll, *130*, 131, 133
Baby Baked Alaskas, *184*, 185
Chocolate Spud, 64, *65*, 66, *67*
Garbage Pound, 214, *215*, 216
Canapés, Throwback Pickled Shrimp, 72, *73*
Cardamom Yogurt Glaze, *100*, 101, 103
Carrot(s)
Mashed Potato Dumpling Soup, 42–43, *44–45*
-Oat Crumble, *100*, 101
Thanksgiving Shepherd's Pie, *240*, 241
Cauliflower, frozen
Cotton Candy Smoothies, *160*, 162
Celery
Thanksgiving Shepherd's Pie, *240*, 241
Cereal Milk Ice Pops, *212*, 213
Champagne Crepes, 226, *227*
Cheddar cheese
& Sage Bread Pudding, 12, *13*
Cheesy Grits with Herbed Browned Butter, *150*, 151
Creamy Broccoli Soup with, "Crackers," 122–23, *123*
Fish & Tot Sandwiches, 58, *59*, 60
Where's the Beet Patty Melts, 110–11, *112–13*
Cheese
All-the-Veggies Shakshuka, 114–15, *116–17*
Bagel French Onion Soup, *22*, 23
Board Pinwheels, 246, *247*
Ciao, Arancini, *46*, 47
Clear-Out-the-Fridge Pasta Salad with Charred Tomato Dressing, 48, *49*
Corned Beef Egg Rolls, *228*, 229
Drawer Soufflés, *142*, 143
Greek Salad, 14–15, *16–17*
Marinated Stuffed Olives, 136, *137*
Mixed-Mushroom Quiche, 144–45, *145*
No-Frills Frittata, 98, *99*
Parmesan Cream Scalloped Potatoes, 152, *153*
Parmesan Rind Cacio e Pepe, 158, *159*
Pizza for Breakfast Sandwiches, *18*, 19, 21
Roasted Squash Bread Salad, 6, *7*, 8
Thanksgiving Shepherd's Pie, *240*, 241
Where's the Beet Patty Melts, 110–11, *112–13*
Cheese, shredded
Any-Season Savory Tart, 118–19, *119*
Buffalo Chicken Bean Dip, 36, *37*
Butternut Squash Quesadillas, 124–25, *126–27*
Cheddar & Sage Bread Pudding, 12, *13*
Cornbread Skillet Sloppy Joes, 32, *33*
Creamy Broccoli Soup with Cheddar "Crackers," 122–23, *123*
Deluxe Grilled, Sandwiches with Onion Jam, *154*, 155
Fish & Tot Sandwiches, 58, *59*, 60
Grilled Pulled Pork Burritos, 86, *87*, 88, *89*
Grits with Herbed Browned Butter, *150*, 151
Hamburger Junior VP, 80, *81*
Hot (Damn) Seafood Dip with Crackers, *74*, 75
(I'm So) Stuffed Shells, *120*, 121
Pot Roast & Potato Pizza, 248–49, *250–51*
Pretzel-Crumb Cheese Ball, 194, *195*, *196–97*
Stuffed Zucchini "Subs," 156–57, *157*
Cheese Cracker-Fried Chicken Sandwiches, 198, *199*, 200
Cheesy Grits with Herbed Browned Butter, *150*, 151
Cherry(ies)
Retro Ambrosia Salad, *164*, 165
Cherry liqueur
The Pink Lady, 177, *179*
Chicken
alla Vodka with Anchovy Breadcrumbs, 174, *175*, 176
Bone Soup with Rice, *38*, 39
Buffalo, Bean Dip, 36, *37*
Cheese Cracker-Fried, Sandwiches, 198, *199*, 200
Mimi's, & Rice Casserole, *52*, 53
Waldorf, Salad Lettuce Cups, *90*, 91
Chicken stock (low-sodium)
Coffee-Glazed Pork Ribs, 204–5, *206–7*
Grilled Pulled Pork Burritos, 86, *87*, 88, *89*
Mimi's Chicken & Rice Casserole, *52*, 53
Sausage, Beans, 'n' Greens, 76–77, *78–79*
Chilaquiles, 188, *190–91*
Chili pepper(s)
Maple Syrup, Sauce, 58, *59*, 60
Chipotle in adobo
Grilled Pulled Pork Burritos, 86, *87*, 88, *89*
Surf & Turf Tacos, 92–93, *94–95*

Chives
Creamy Broccoli Soup with Cheddar "Crackers," 122–23, *123*
Pretzel-Crumb Cheese Ball, 194, *195*, *196–97*
Smoked Salmon Omelet for One, 166, *167*
Tartar Sauce, 70–71, *71*
Tuna Salad Cakes, 70–71, *71*
Waldorf Chicken Salad Lettuce Cups, *90*, 91
Chocolate
Drizzle, 214, *215*, 216
Peppermint Hot, Cookies, 252, *253*
Spud Cake, 64, *65*, 66, *67*
Trick-or-Treat Fudge, 236, *238–39*
Ciao, Arancini, *46*, 47
Cilantro
All-the-Veggies Shakshuka, 114–15, *116–17*
Butternut Squash Quesadillas, 124–25, *126–27*
Chicken Bone Soup with Rice, *38*, 39
Grilled Pulled Pork Burritos, 86, *87*, 88, *89*
Jalapeño, & Lime Dressing, 169, *170–71*
Rice, 86, *87*, 88, *89*
Savory Quinoa Porridge with Mushrooms, *108*, 109
Surf & Turf Tacos, 92–93, *94–95*
Yogurt Sauce, 54, *55*, 56
Clear-Out-the-Fridge Pasta Salad with Charred Tomato Dressing, 48, *49*
Clementines
Retro Ambrosia Salad, *164*, 165
Cocktails
Cranberry Sauce, *244*, 245
Hurricane Granitas, *220*, 221
The Last Pour, 217, *219*
The Pink Lady, 177, *179*
Squeaky Clean Martinis, 222, *223*
Cocoa powder
Chocolate Spud Cake, 64, *65*, 66, *67*
Mocha Iced Latte, *192*, 193
Peppermint Hot Chocolate Cookies, 252, *253*
Coconut, shredded
Retro Ambrosia Salad, *164*, 165
Coffee
Bottom of the Pot Mocha Iced Latte, *192*, 193
-Glazed Pork Ribs, 204–5, *206–7*
Cookies, Peppermint Hot Chocolate, 252, *253*
Cornbread Skillet Sloppy Joes, 32, *33*
Corned Beef Egg Rolls, *228*, 229
Cornmeal grits
Cheesy Grits with Herbed Browned Butter, *150*, 151
Lemon Polenta Flapjacks, 61, *62*, *63*
Cotija cheese
Chilaquiles, 188, *190–91*
Cotton Candy Smoothies, *160*, 162
Cranberry Sauce Cocktail, *244*, 245
Cream, heavy
Chocolate Drizzle, 214, *215*, 216
Jammy Whip, 2
Mixed-Mushroom Quiche, 144–45, *145*
Mushroom Gravy, 24
Cream cheese
Aunt Jenny's Sweet Potato Cake Roll, *130*, 131, 133
Hot (Damn) Seafood Dip with Crackers, *74*, 75
Pretzel-Crumb Cheese Ball, 194, *195*, *196–97*
Smoked Salmon Omelet for One, 166, *167*
Throwback Pickled Shrimp Canapés, 72, *73*
Creamy Broccoli Soup with Cheddar "Crackers," 122–23, *123*
Crepes, Champagne, 226, *227*
pan for, 226
Crescent rolls
Pull-Apart Pigs in a Quilt, *234*, 235
Croutons, Everything, 9, *10–11*
Crumble Topping, Carrot-Oat, *100*, 101

D

Deluxe Grilled Cheese Sandwiches with Onion Jam, *154*, 155
Dill, fresh
Mashed Potato Dumpling Soup, 42–43, *44–45*
Nut-Crusted Fish, *202*, 203
Waldorf Chicken Salad Lettuce Cups, *90*, 91
Dips
Buffalo Chicken Bean, 36, *37*
Hot (Damn) Seafood, with Crackers, *74*, 75
Doughnuts, Berry-Glazed Sour Cream, 180, *182–83*
Drizzle
Chocolate, 214, *215*, 216
White Chocolate, 252, *253*

E

Eat Your Veg Muffins with Carrot-Oat Crumble, *100*, 101, 103
Eggplant
All-the-Veggies Shakshuka, 114–15, *116–17*
Egg Rolls, Corned Beef, *228*, 229
Egg(s)
All-the-Veggies Shakshuka, 114–15, *116–17*
Aunt Jenny's Sweet Potato Cake Roll, *130*, 131, 133
Baked French Toast, 2, *3*
Berry-Glazed Sour Cream Doughnuts, 180, *182–83*
Cheese Drawer Soufflés, *142*, 143
Chilaquiles, 188, *190–91*
Latke Breakfast Hash with Greens, 242, *243*
Mixed-Mushroom Quiche, 144–45, *145*
No-Frills Frittata, 98, *99*
Old-School Ham Salad, 232, *233*
Peppermint Hot Chocolate Cookies, 252, *253*
Pizza for Breakfast Sandwiches, *18*, 19, 21

Pound Cake, 214, *215*, 216
Smoked Salmon Omelet for One, 166, *167*
Spaghetti Pie, Oh My! *50*, 51
Tuna Salad Cakes with Tartar Sauce, 70–71, *71*
Veggie Ramen Salad, 104, *105*, 106, *107*
Egg whites
Meringue, *184*, 185
The Pink Lady, 177, *179*
Yesterday's Crispy Rice Cakes, 40, *41*
Egg yolks
Caesar Dressing, 9, *10–11*
Enchilada sauce, store-bought
Chilaquiles, 188, *190–91*
Everything Croutons, 9, *10–11*

F

Fennel
Thanksgiving Shepherd's Pie, *240*, 241
Throwback Pickled Shrimp Canapés, 72, *73*
Waldorf Chicken Salad Lettuce Cups, *90*, 91
Fish
& Tot Sandwiches, 58, *59*, 60
Nut-Crusted, *202*, 203
Surf & Turf Tacos, 92–93, *94–95*
Tuna Salad Cakes with Tartar Sauce, 70–71, *71*
Fondue, All-the-Cheeses Spread &, 138, *140–41*
Fontina cheese
Any-Season Savory Tart, 118–19, *119*
French Toast, Baked, 2, *3*
Frittata, No Frills, 98, *99*
Frosting, Chocolate, 64, *65*, 66, *67*
Fudge, Trick-or-Treat, 236, *238–39*
Furikake
about, 40
Yesterday's Crispy Rice Cakes, 40, *41*

G

Garbage Pound Cake, 214, *215*, 216
Gin
The Pink Lady, 177, *179*
Squeaky Clean Martinis, 222, *223*
Ginger, fresh
Chicken Bone Soup with Rice, *38*, 39
Onion Jam, 155
Glaze
Berry, 180, *182–83*
Cardamom Yogurt, *100*, 101, 103
Coffee, 204–5, *206–7*
Goat cheese
All-the-Veggies Shakshuka, 114–15, *116–17*
Marinated Stuffed Olives, 136, *137*
Pretzel-Crumb Cheese Ball, 194, *195*, *196–97*
gochujang
Veggie Ramen Salad, 104, *105*, 106, *107*
Gravy, Creamy Mushroom, 24
Greek to Me, New to You Pita Salad Bowls, 14–15, *16–17*
Greens
Roasted Squash Bread Salad, 6, *7*, 8
Sausage, Beans, 'n,' 76–77, *78–79*
See also Kale; *specific greens*
Grilled Pulled Pork Burritos, 86, *87*, 88, *89*
Grits, Cheesy, with Herbed Browned Butter, *150*, 151
Gruyère cheese
Bagel French Onion Soup, *22*, 23
Thanksgiving Shepherd's Pie, *240*, 241

H

Half-and-half
Baked French Toast, 2, *3*
Halloumi cheese
Greek Salad, 14–15, *16–17*
Halloween candy
Trick-or-Treat Fudge, 236, *238–39*
Hamburger Junior VP, 80, *81*
Ham Salad, Old-School, 232, *233*
Hash, Latke Breakfast, 242, *243*
Herbs, fresh
All-the-Cheeses Spread & Fondue, 138, *140–41*
Clear-Out-the-Fridge Pasta Salad with Charred Tomato Dressing, 48, *49*
Herbed Browned Butter, *150*, 151
(I'm So) Stuffed Shells, *120*, 121
Throwback Pickled Shrimp Canapés, 72, *73*
Horseradish
Buttermilk, Mashed Potatoes, 173
Hot (Damn) Seafood Dip with Crackers, *74*, 75
Hot dogs
Pull-Apart Pigs in a Quilt, *234*, 235
Hurricane Granitas, *220*, 221

I

Ice cream
Baby Baked Alaskas, *184*, 185
(I'm So) Stuffed Shells, *120*, 121

J

Jalapeño(s)
Cilantro, & Lime Dressing, 169, *170–71*
Surf & Turf Tacos, 92–93, *94–95*
Jam
Onion, 155
Rescue-Those-Berries Preserves, 128, *128*, *129*
Jammy Whip, 2, *3*

K

Kale
Caesar with Everything Croutons, 9, *10–11*
Roasted Squash Bread Salad, 6, *7*, 8
Sausage, Beans, 'n' Greens, 76–77, *78–79*
Surf & Turf Tacos, 92–93, *94–95*
Ketchup
Thousand Island Dressing, 169, *170–71*

L

Last Pour, The, 217, *219*
Latke Breakfast Hash with Greens, 242, *243*
Latte, Mocha Iced, *192*, 193
Lemon
  Breaded Pork Chops, 28–30, *29*
  Polenta Flapjacks, 61, *62*, *63*
Lettuce
  Cheese Cracker-Fried Chicken Sandwiches, 198, *199*, 200
  Waldorf Chicken Salad, Cups, *90*, 91
Lime
  Jalapeño, Cilantro, &, Dressing, 169, *170–71*
  Sour Cream, 124–25, *126–27*

M

Maple Syrup Chili Sauce, 58, *59*, 60
Marinade, 136
Marinated Stuffed Olives, 136, *137*
Marshmallows
  Retro Ambrosia Salad, *164*, 165
Martinis, Squeaky Clean, 222, *223*
Mashed Potato(es)
  Buttermilk Horseradish, 173
  Dumpling Soup, 42–43, *44–45*
  Saucy Swedish Meatballs, 24–25, *26–27*
  Thanksgiving Shepherd's Pie, *240*, 241
Mayonnaise
  Hot (Damn) Seafood Dip with Crackers, *74*, 75
  Jalapeño, Cilantro, & Lime Dressing, 169, *170–71*
  Old-School Ham Salad, 232, *233*
  Tangy Ranch Dressing, 168, *170–71*
  Tartar Sauce, 70–71, *71*
  Thousand Island Dressing, 169, *170–71*
  Throwback Pickled Shrimp Canapés, 72, *73*
  Waldorf Chicken Salad Lettuce Cups, *90*, 91
  Where's the Beet Patty Melts, 110–11, *112–13*
Mean Bean Burgers with Saffron Yogurt Sauce, 54, *55*, 56
Meatballs
  Saucy Swedish, 24–25, *26–27*
  Stuffed Zucchini "Subs," 156–57, *157*
Meringue, *184*, 185
Milk, nondairy
  Mocha Iced Latte, *192*, 193
Milk, whole
  Aunt Jenny's Sweet Potato Cake Roll, *130*, 131, 133
  Cereal Milk Ice Pops, *212*, 213
  Champagne Crepes, 226, *227*
  Cheddar & Sage Bread Pudding, 12, *13*
  Cheese Drawer Soufflés, *142*, 143
  No-Frills Frittata, 98, *99*
  Saucy Swedish Meatballs, 24–25, *26–27*
  Stuffed Zucchini "Subs," 156–57, *157*
  Tuna Salad Cakes with Tartar Sauce, 70–71, *71*
Mimi's Chicken & Rice Casserole, *52*, 53
Miso Butter, 155
Mixed-Mushroom Quiche, 144–45, *145*
Mocha Ice Cubes, *192*, 193
Monterey Jack cheese
  Buffalo Chicken Bean Dip, 36, *37*
Mozzarella cheese
  Clear-Out-the-Fridge Pasta Salad with Charred Tomato Dressing, 48, *49*
  Corned Beef Egg Rolls, *228*, 229
  (I'm So) Stuffed Shells, *120*, 121
Muffins, Eat Your Veg, with Carrot-Oat Crumble, *100*, 101, 103
Mushroom(s)
  Gravy, 24
  Mimi's Chicken & Rice Casserole, *52*, 53
  Mixed-, Quiche, 144–45, *145*
  Savory Quinoa Porridge with, *108*, 109

N

No-Frills Frittata, 98, *99*
Nut(s)
  -Crusted Fish, *202*, 203
  Savory Quinoa Porridge with Mushrooms, *108*, 109
  Waldorf Chicken Salad Lettuce Cups, *90*, 91

O

Oat(s) (rolled oats)
  Carrot-, Crumble, *100*, 101
  Mean Bean Burgers with Saffron Yogurt Sauce, 54, *55*, 56
  Where's the Beet Patty Melts, 110–11, *112–13*
Old-School Ham Salad, 232, *233*
Olive(s)
  Marinated Stuffed, 136, *137*
  Squeaky Clean Martinis, 222, *223*
Onion(s)
  Any-Season Savory Tart, 118–19, *119*
  Bagel French, Soup, *22*, 23
  Butternut Squash Quesadillas, 124–25, *126–27*
  Chilaquiles, 188, *190–91*
  Greek Salad, 14–15, *16–17*
  Saucy Swedish Meatballs, 24–25, *26–27*
  Sausage, Beans, 'n' Greens, 76–77, *78–79*
  Savory Quinoa Porridge with Mushrooms, *108*, 109
  Something-Borrowed Bourguignon, 82–83, *84–85*
  Surf & Turf Tacos, 92–93, *94–95*
Orange juice
  Hurricane Granitas, *220*, 221

P

Pancakes
  Lemon Polenta Flapjacks, 61, *62*, *63*
Parmesan cheese
  Cream, 152, *153*

Pizza for Breakfast Sandwiches, *18*, 19, 21
Rind Cacio e Pepe, 158, *159*
rinds, collecting and storing, 152
Savory Tart crust, 118–19, *119*
Parsley, fresh
All-the-Veggies Shakshuka, 114–15, *116–17*
Bagel French Onion Soup, *22*, 23
Ciao, Arancini, *46*, 47
Dressing, Greek Salad, 14–15, *16–17*
Herbed Browned Butter, *150*, 151
Mashed Potato Dumpling Soup, 42–43, *44–45*
Mean Bean Burgers with Saffron Yogurt Sauce, 54, *55*, 56
Mimi's Chicken & Rice Casserole, *52*, 53
Nut-Crusted Fish, *202*, 203
Pot Roast & Potato Pizza, 248–49, *250–51*
Pull-Apart Pigs in a Quilt, *234*, 235
Sausage, Beans, 'n' Greens, 76–77, *78–79*
Something-Borrowed Bourguignon, 82–83, *84–85*
Waldorf Chicken Salad Lettuce Cups, *90*, 91
Passion fruit juice
Hurricane Granitas, *220*, 221
Pasta
Chicken alla Vodka with Anchovy Breadcrumbs, 174, *175*, 176
Clear-Out-the-Fridge, Salad with Charred Tomato Dressing, 48, *49*
Hamburger Junior VP, 80, *81*
(I'm So) Stuffed Shells, *120*, 121
Parmesan Rind Cacio e Pepe, 158, *159*
Spaghetti Pie, Oh My! *50*, 51
Peppercorns
Blue Cheese Buttah, 146, *147*, *148–49*
Pepper Jack cheese
Grilled Pulled Pork Burritos, 86, *87*, 88, *89*
Hot (Damn) Seafood Dip with Crackers, *74*, 75
Peppermint Hot Chocolate Cookies, 252, *253*
Pepper(s), red bell
All-the-Veggies Shakshuka, 114–15, *116–17*
Hamburger Junior VP, 80, *81*
Latke Breakfast Hash, 242, *243*
Pepper(s), roasted
All-the-Cheeses Spread & Fondue, 138, *140–41*
Pickle-Brined Sauerbraten, 208, *209*, 210, *211*
Pie Crust, 144
Pineapple
Retro Ambrosia Salad, *164*, 165
Pinwheels, Cheese Board, 246, *247*
Pistachio(s)
Retro Ambrosia Salad, *164*, 165
Pita Salad Bowls, 14–15, *16–17*
Pizza
for Breakfast Sandwiches, *18*, 19, 21
Dough, 248–49
Pot Roast & Potato, 248–49, *250–51*
Polenta Flapjacks, Lemon, 61, *62*, *63*
Pork
Coffee-Glazed, Ribs, 204–5, *206–7*
Grilled Pulled, Burritos, 86, *87*, 88, *89*
Lemony Breaded, Chops, 28–30, *29*
Stuffed Zucchini "Subs," 156–57, *157*
Porridge, Savory Quinoa, with Mushrooms, *108*, 109
Potato chips
Chocolate Spud Cake, 64, *65*, 66, *67*
Potato(es)
Chocolate Spud Cake, 64, *65*, 66, *67*
Creamy Broccoli Soup with Cheddar "Crackers," 122–23, *123*
Parmesan Cream Scalloped, 152, *153*
Pot Roast &, Pizza, 248–49, *250–51*
Something-Borrowed Bourguignon, 82–83, *84–85*
See also Mashed Potato(es)
Pot Roast & Potato Pizza, 248–49, *250–51*
Pretzel-Crumb Cheese Ball, 194, *195*, *196–97*
Prosciutto
Pizza for Breakfast Sandwiches, *18*, 19, 21
Puff pastry
Cheese Board Pinwheels, 246, *247*
Pull-Apart Pigs in a Quilt, *234*, 235

Q

Quesadillas, Butternut Squash, 124–25, *126–27*
Quiche, Mixed-Mushroom, 144–45, *145*
Quinoa
Savory Porridge with Mushrooms, *108*, 109

R

Radish(es)
Chilaquiles, 188, *190–91*
Ramen noodles
Veggie, Salad, 104, *105*, 106, *107*
Rescue-Those-Berries Preserves, *128*, 128, *129*
Retro Ambrosia Salad, *164*, 165
Rice
Chicken Bone Soup with, *38*, 39
Ciao, Arancini, *46*, 47
Cilantro, 86, *87*, 88, *89*
Mimi's Chicken &, Casserole, *52*, 53
Yesterday's Crispy, Cakes, 40, *41*
Ricotta cheese
(I'm So) Stuffed Shells, *120*, 121
Lemon Polenta Flapjacks, 61, *62*, *63*
Marinated Stuffed Olives, 136, *137*
No-Frills Frittata, 98, *99*
Pizza for Breakfast Sandwiches, *18*, 19, 21
Ritz crackers
Tuna Salad Cakes, 70–71, *71*

Roasted Squash Bread Salad, 6, *7*, 8
Romaine lettuce
  Greek Salad, 14–15, *16–17*
Rosemary, fresh
  Herbed Browned Butter, *150*, 151
  Mixed-Mushroom Quiche, 144–45, *145*
  Pickle-Brined Sauerbraten, 208, *209*, 210, *211*
  Something-Borrowed Bourguignon, 82–83, *84–85*
Rum
  Hurricane Granitas, *220*, 221

S

Saffron Yogurt Sauce, 54, *55*, 56
Sage
  Cheddar &, Bread Pudding, 12, *13*
  Herbed Browned Butter, *150*, 151
Salad
  Clear-Out-the-Fridge Pasta, with Charred Tomato Dressing, 48, *49*
  Greek, 14–15, *16–17*
  Kale Caesar, 9, *10–11*
  Old-School Ham, 232, *233*
  Roasted Squash Bread, 6, *7*, 8
  Veggie Ramen, 104, *105*, 106, *107*
  Waldorf Chicken, Lettuce Cups, *90*, 91
Salad dressings, 14–15, *15*, *16–17*
  Bacon-Dripping Vinaigrette, 6, *7*, 8
  Caesar, 9, *10–11*
  Charred Tomato, 48, *49*
  Jalapeño, Cilantro, & Lime, 169, *170–71*
  Tangy Ranch, 168, *170–71*
  tangy sour cream-mayo, *90*, 91
  Thousand Island, 169, *170–71*
Salmon, smoked
  Caesar Dressing, 9, *10–11*
  Kale Caesar, 9, *10–11*
  Omelet for One, 166, *167*
Sandwiches
  Cheese Cracker-Fried Chicken, 198, *199*, 200
  Deluxe Grilled Cheese, with Onion Jam, *154*, 155
  Fish & Tot, 58, *59*, 60
  Pizza for Breakfast, *18*, 19, 21
  Where's the Beet Patty Melts, 110–11, *112–13*
Sauce
  Maple Syrup Chili, 58, *59*, 60
  Tartar, 70–71, *71*
  Yogurt, 54, *55*, 56
Saucy Swedish Meatballs, 24–25, *26–27*
Sauerbraten, Pickle-Brined, 208, *209*, 210, *211*
Sausage
  Beans, 'n' Greens, 76–77, *78–79*
  Latke Breakfast Hash with Greens, 242, *243*
Savory Quinoa Porridge with Mushrooms, *108*, 109
Scallion(s)
  Tartar Sauce, 70–71, *71*
  Tuna Salad Cakes, 70–71, *71*
Seafood
  Hot (Damn), Dip with Crackers, *74*, 75
  Throwback Pickled Shrimp Canapés, 72, *73*
Shakshuka, All-the-Veggies, 114–15, *116–17*
Shepherd's Pie, Thanksgiving, *240*, 241
Sherry
  Any-Season Savory Tart, 118–19, *119*
Shrimp
  how to cook raw shrimp, 72
  Throwback Pickled, Canapés, 72, *73*
Sloppy Joes, Cornbread Skillet, 32, *33*
Smoothie, Cotton Candy, *160*, 162
Something-Borrowed Bourguignon, 82–83, *84–85*
Soufflés, Cheese Drawer, *142*, 143
Soup
  Bagel French Onion, *22*, 23
  Chicken Bone, with Rice, *38*, 39
  Creamy Broccoli, with Cheddar "Crackers," 122–23, *123*
  Mashed Potato Dumpling, 42–43, *44–45*
Sour cream
  Aunt Jenny's Sweet Potato Cake Roll, *130*, 131, 133
  Berry-Glazed, Doughnuts, 180, *182–83*
  Chilaquiles, 188, *190–91*
  Creamy Broccoli Soup with Cheddar "Crackers," 122–23, *123*
  Garbage Pound Cake, 214, *215*, 216
  Hamburger Junior VP, 80, *81*
  Hot (Damn) Seafood Dip with Crackers, *74*, 75
  Lime, 124–25, *126–27*
  Tangy Ranch Dressing, 168, *170–71*
  Waldorf Chicken Salad Lettuce Cups, *90*, 91
Spaghetti Pie, Oh My! *50*, 51
Spinach, fresh
  Creamy Broccoli Soup with Cheddar "Crackers," 122–23, *123*
Spinach, frozen
  Hot (Damn) Seafood Dip with Crackers, *74*, 75
  (I'm So) Stuffed Shells, *120*, 121
Squash
  Butternut, Quesadillas, 124–25, *126–27*
  Roasted, Bread Salad, 6, *7*, 8
Stew
  Something-Borrowed Bourguignon, 82–83, *84–85*
Stuffed Shells, *120*, 121
Stuffed Zucchini "Subs," 156–57, *157*
Surf & Turf Tacos, 92–93, *94–95*
Sweet potato
  Aunt Jenny's, Cake Roll, *130*, 131, 133
Swiss chard
  Latke Breakfast Hash with Greens, 242, *243*
  Sausage, Beans, 'n' Greens, 76–77, *78–79*

T

Tacos, Surf & Turf, 92–93, *94–95*
Tangy Ranch Dressing, 168, *170–71*
Tarragon, fresh
Blue Cheese Buttah, 146, *147*, *148–49*
Tart, Any-Season Savory, 118–19, *119*
Tater tots
Fish & Tot Sandwiches, 58, *59*, 60
Waffles, 58, *59*, 60
Thanksgiving Shepherd's Pie, *240*, 241
Thousand Island Dressing, 169, *170–71*
Throwback Pickled Shrimp Canapés, 72, *73*
Thyme, fresh
Any-Season Savory Tart, 118–19, *119*
Bagel French Onion Soup, *22*, 23
Cheese Drawer Soufflés, *142*, 143
Herbed Browned Butter, *150*, 151
Mixed-Mushroom Quiche, 144–45, *145*
Pickle-Brined Sauerbraten, 208, *209*, 210, *211*
Saucy Swedish Meatballs, 24–25, *26–27*
Something-Borrowed Bourguignon, 82–83, *84–85*
Tomato(es)
Clear-Out-the-Fridge Pasta Salad with Charred, Dressing, 48, *49*
Tomato paste
All-the-Veggies Shakshuka, 114–15, *116–17*
buying tip, 32
Chicken alla Vodka with Anchovy Breadcrumbs, 174, *175*, 176
Cornbread Skillet Sloppy Joes, 32, *33*
Something-Borrowed Bourguignon, 82–83, *84–85*
Tomato sauce
All-the-Veggies Shakshuka, 114–15, *116–17*
Ciao, Arancini, *46*, 47
Cornbread Skillet Sloppy Joes, 32, *33*
(I'm So) Stuffed Shells, *120*, 121
Tortilla chips
Chilaquiles, 188, *190–91*
Trick-or-Treat Fudge, 236, *238–39*
Tuna Salad Cakes with Tartar Sauce, 70–71, *71*
Turkey
Cornbread Skillet Sloppy Joes, 32, *33*
Thanksgiving Shepherd's Pie, *240*, 241

V

Vegetable stock, low-sodium
Creamy Broccoli Soup with Cheddar "Crackers," 122–23, *123*
Mean Bean Burgers with Saffron Yogurt Sauce, 54, *55*, 56
Where's the Beet Patty Melts, 110–11, *112–13*
Veggies, frozen
Chicken Bone Soup with Rice, *38*, 39
Veggies, raw
Ramen Salad, 104, *105*, 106, *107*
Veggies, roasted or grilled
Clear-Out-the-Fridge Pasta Salad with Charred Tomato Dressing, 48, *49*
how to roast, 49
No-Frills Frittata, 98, *99*
Vermouth
Saucy Swedish Meatballs, 24–25, *26–27*
Squeaky Clean Martinis, 222, *223*
Vinaigrette, Bacon-Dripping, 6, *7*, 8
Vodka
Chicken alla, with Anchovy Breadcrumbs, 174, *175*
Squeaky Clean Martinis, 222, *223*

W

Waffles, tater tot, 58, *59*, 60
Waldorf Chicken Salad Lettuce Cups, *90*, 91
Where's the Beet Patty Melts, 110–11, *112–13*
Whipped topping
Retro Ambrosia Salad, *164*, 165
Who Left the Chip Bag Open?
Chilaquiles, 188, *190–91*
Wine (red)
The Last Pour, 217, *219*
Pickle-Brined Sauerbraten, 208, *209*, 210, *211*
Something-Borrowed Bourguignon, 82–83, *84–85*
Wine (white)
All-the-Cheeses Spread & Fondue, 138, *140–41*
Hamburger Junior VP, 80, *81*
The Last Pour, 217, *219*
Mimi's Chicken & Rice Casserole, *52*, 53
Sausage, Beans, 'n' Greens, 76–77, *78–79*

Y

Yesterday's Crispy Rice Cakes, 40, *41*
Yogurt
Cardamom, Glaze, *100*, 101, 103
Cereal Milk Ice Pops, *212*, 213
Sauce, 54, *55*, 56

Z

Za'atar
Pita Bowls, 14–15, *15*, *16–17*
substitutions for, 15
Zucchini
Eat Your Veg Muffins with Carrot-Oat Crumble, *100*, 101, 103
Stuffed, "Subs," 156–57, *157*

About the Author

TIFFANI THIESSEN is an actor and author who also knows a thing or two about good food. Most people know her as America's Sweetheart Kelly Kapowski from *Saved by the Bell* and Valerie Malone from *Beverly Hills, 90210*. But when she's not appearing in an Emmy-nominated series (*Alexa & Katie*), hosting an MTV viral sensation (*Deliciousness*), or starring in her own Food Network show (*Dinner at Tiffani's*), she's thinking up playful and tasty new recipes with a twist of nostalgia. You can find more of her simple-yet-polished dishes in her critically acclaimed first cookbook, *Pull Up a Chair*. She lives in Los Angeles with her husband, daughter, and son.

RACHEL HOLTZMAN is a *New York Times* bestselling coauthor who loves partnering with people who appreciate hard work, speaking from the heart, and the importance of a good snack—which is why this is her second collaboration with Tiffani.